First World War
and Army of Occupation
War Diary
France, Belgium and Germany

57 DIVISION
172 Infantry Brigade
King's (Liverpool Regiment)
9th Battalion
1 February 1918 - 10 May 1919

WO95/2985/2

The Naval & Military Press Ltd
www.nmarchive.com
Published in association with The National Archives

Published by

The Naval & Military Press Ltd

Unit 10 Ridgewood Industrial Park,

Uckfield, East Sussex,

TN22 5QE England

Tel: +44 (0) 1825 749494

www.naval-military-press.com

www.nmarchive.com

This diary has been reprinted in facsimile from the original. Any imperfections are inevitably reproduced and the quality may fall short of modern type and cartographic standards.

© **Crown Copyright**
Images reproduced by permission of The National Archives, London, England, 2015.

Contents

Document type	Place/Title	Date From	Date To
Heading	WO95/2985/2 57 Divn 172 Inf Brig 1/9 King's Liverpool Regt 1918 Feb-1919 May		
Heading	57 Division 172 Bde 1/9 Bn Kings Liverpool Regt 1918 Feb-1919 May		
War Diary	Steinwerke	01/02/1918	01/02/1918
War Diary	Waterlands Camp	03/02/1918	06/02/1918
War Diary	Armentieres Sector	09/02/1918	15/02/1918
War Diary	Estaires	16/02/1918	25/02/1918
War Diary	Le Sart	01/03/1918	09/03/1918
War Diary	Estaires	10/03/1918	20/03/1918
War Diary	In The Line	21/03/1918	31/03/1918
Heading	57th Division 172nd Infantry Brigade War Diary 9th Battalion The King's Liverpool Regiment April 1918		
War Diary	Estaires	01/04/1918	01/04/1918
War Diary	Haverskerque	02/04/1918	02/04/1918
War Diary	Doullens	03/04/1918	03/04/1918
War Diary	Sus-St. Leger	04/04/1918	05/04/1918
War Diary	Warluzel	06/04/1918	08/04/1918
War Diary	Thievres	09/04/1918	12/04/1918
War Diary	Sombrin	13/04/1918	13/04/1918
War Diary	Beaucamp Rav	14/04/1918	14/04/1918
War Diary	Henu	15/04/1918	05/05/1918
War Diary	Gommecourt Wood	06/05/1918	14/05/1918
War Diary	In The Line	14/05/1918	24/05/1918
War Diary	Beer Trch	25/05/1918	29/05/1918
War Diary	Rurt Trench	29/05/1918	31/05/1918
War Diary	Gommecourt	01/06/1918	07/06/1918
War Diary	In The Line	09/06/1918	15/06/1918
War Diary	Rossignol Farm	15/06/1918	15/06/1918
War Diary	Chateau De La Haie	16/06/1918	21/06/1918
War Diary	Rossignol Farm	21/06/1918	23/06/1918
War Diary	In The Line	23/06/1918	30/06/1918
Miscellaneous	Appendix A To War Diary for The month June 1918		
War Diary	Line	01/07/1918	02/07/1918
War Diary	Authie	02/07/1918	30/07/1918
War Diary	Arras	31/07/1918	31/07/1918
Miscellaneous	Appendix A To War Diary for July 1918		
War Diary	Arras	01/08/1918	20/08/1918
War Diary	Bailleul	20/08/1918	21/08/1918
War Diary	Fosseux	22/08/1918	22/08/1918
War Diary	Boucquemaison	23/08/1918	23/08/1918
War Diary	Barly	24/08/1918	25/08/1918
War Diary	Bellacourt	26/08/1918	26/08/1918
War Diary	Henin	27/08/1918	27/08/1918
War Diary	Humber Redoubt	28/08/1918	28/08/1918
War Diary	Fag Alley Etc	28/08/1918	31/08/1918
War Diary	Henin	01/09/1918	01/09/1918
War Diary	Hendicourt Trench	02/09/1918	16/09/1918
War Diary	Bullecourt	17/09/1918	18/09/1918
War Diary	Bailleulmont	19/09/1918	19/09/1918

War Diary	Lagnicourt	25/09/1918	27/09/1918
War Diary	Bailleulmont	20/09/1918	25/09/1918
War Diary	Bourlon	28/09/1918	28/09/1918
War Diary	Bourlon Wood	28/09/1918	28/09/1918
War Diary	Anneux	28/09/1918	30/09/1918
War Diary	S Of Cambrai	30/09/1918	30/09/1918
War Diary	Cambrai	01/10/1918	01/10/1918
War Diary	La Folie Wood District	02/10/1918	03/10/1918
War Diary	La Folie Wood District Cambrai	03/10/1918	04/10/1918
War Diary	Proville	05/10/1918	06/10/1918
War Diary	S.W. Of Cambrai	07/10/1918	09/10/1918
War Diary	Cantaing Trenches Anneux	10/10/1918	11/10/1918
War Diary	Near Inchy	12/10/1918	12/10/1918
War Diary	Douvrin	13/10/1918	14/10/1918
War Diary	Le Maisnil	14/10/1918	17/10/1918
War Diary	Lille	17/10/1918	20/10/1918
War Diary	Lille Ascq	21/10/1918	21/10/1918
War Diary	Ascq Willems	22/10/1918	22/10/1918
War Diary	Willems	23/10/1918	24/10/1918
War Diary	Froyennes	24/10/1918	28/10/1918
War Diary	Cornet	29/10/1918	30/10/1918
Miscellaneous	The 9th King's		
War Diary	Hellemmes	30/10/1918	03/12/1918
War Diary	Carvin	04/12/1918	04/12/1918
War Diary	Etrun	05/12/1918	09/12/1918
War Diary	Y Hutments	10/12/1918	31/12/1918
War Diary	Maroeuil Y Hutments L2C And D	01/01/1919	31/01/1919
Miscellaneous	Extract from The Liverpool Daily Post & Mercury	07/01/1919	07/01/1919
War Diary	Y Hutments Maroeuil	01/02/1919	15/03/1919
War Diary	Marouel	16/03/1919	10/05/1919
Heading	57 Division 172 Bde 2/9 Bn Kings Liverpool Regt 1915 Sep-1916 Feb 1917 Feb-1918 Jan		

WO 95 2985/2

57 Divn. 172 Inf Brig
1/9 King's Liverpool Regt
1918 Feb — 1919 May

57 DIVISION

172 BDE

1/9 BN KINGS LIVERPOOL REGT

1918 FEB — 1919 MAR

FROM 55 DIV 165 BDE

(Absorbed 2/9 Bn 1918 Feb)

WAR DIARY
INTELLIGENCE SUMMARY

9th Battalion, Kings (Liverpool Regt.) T.F.

Army Form C. 2118.

Place	Date	Hour	Summary of Events and Information	Remarks and references to Appendices
STEINNERKE	Feby 2/18		We arrived at Steinnerke about 4.30 p.m. on the 29th Jan. and remained in the trenches we were taken to "Stanton's Camp" and remained here until 2nd Feby when we proceeded to join the Battalion in Waterlands Camp, the 2/9 having come out of the line to this camp.	
WATERLANDS CAMP	3		The following days were spent in reorganising the whole Battalion.	
"	4			
"	5		On the 5th inst the Baths were allotted to the unit.	
"	6		All ranks appear to be settling down to the new conditions & working together amicably. Members of old 49th apparently very keen to imbue the new comrades with the traditions of the old Battalion and to keep alive its fighting spirit and smartness.	
ARMENTIERES SECTOR	9		The Battalion moved into the line relieving the 2/10 Kings Regt in the Armentieres Sector. During the next 3 days everything passed off very quietly.	
	10			
			On the evening of our 4th day Relief took place.	
	13		On the 13th inst the Battalion was relieved by the 18th and retired	
EMIRES	14		to billets and proceeded to Pillivart in EMIRES. The Battalion spent up to 18th inst in cleaning up etc.	13.F

WAR DIARY
or
INTELLIGENCE SUMMARY

Army Form C. 2118.

(Erase heading not required.)

Instructions regarding War Diaries and Intelligence Summaries are contained in F. S. Regs., Part II. and the Staff Manual respectively. Title pages will be prepared in manuscript.

Place	Date	Hour	Summary of Events and Information	Remarks and references to Appendices
ESTAIRES	17		The Battalion was called up to furnish working parties working parties each night to be supplied by the duties of a new Coy. system. One Coy. each day to supply no working parties. One Coy. each day to supply the training of the Coy.	
			The enemy in making sulted artillery on to billets caused some damage. Gas Gas Shells fired – Russian reserve trenches. Shelling & bombing – Red Russian trench.	
	23		Relief of 5th Batt. Bucks Hussars to dull dawn to Estaires Came in Reid Camb crossed roughly during dark dawn 6:15 hours.	
	24		Relief of one Coy. appeared to be very fair cover. No casualties was received. One Officer Lt. Chris had been wounded by military fire and two O.R.'s Park had been wounded by military fire and Lce/Cpl Ruskel clearly & gallantly carried on during the raid which was successfully carried through.	
	25		The right of the 30th June 1916. By B. 23 & 2 succeeding	

WAR DIARY
or
INTELLIGENCE SUMMARY.

(Erase heading not required.) 1/5 9th Bn. "The King's (Liverpool Regt)" T.F.

Army Form C. 2118.

Instructions regarding War Diaries and Intelligence Summaries are contained in F. S. Regs., Part II. and the Staff Manual respectively. Title pages will be prepared in manuscript.

Place	Date	Hour	Summary of Events and Information	Remarks and references to Appendices
ESTAIRES	25.		days to hold were allotted to the battalions. Intimation was received about this time that the Divisional General would inspect the Battalion on the 1st March. During this period to date all amount was only moderate	

July 25th 1916.

J.W.Burn
Lieut Colonel Comdg
1/5 B.n "The Kings (Liverpool Regt)" T.F.

Army Form C. 2118.

WAR DIARY
or
INTELLIGENCE SUMMARY.
(Erase heading not required.)

9th Bn. The King's (Liverpool Regiment)

Vol 14

Place	Date	Hour	Summary of Events and Information	Remarks and references to Appendices
Le Sart	1/3/18		The Battalion left the Huttments at Estaires & moved into Billets at Le Sart for a fortnights training	
"	2/3/18 3/3/18 4/3/18 5/3/18		The following programme of training was carried out - Musketry Extended Order Drill Physical Bayonet & Company Drill Battalion was inspected during the forenoon by the Commanding Officer. During the afternoon the usual training was proceeded with	
"	6/3/18		The G.O.C. 57th Division inspected the Battalion. The Battalion presented a very smart appearance on parade & received an excellent report from the G.O.C.	
"	7/3/18 8/3/18		The usual training was carried out on these days	
"	9/3/18		Orders were received at 1.40 am to move to Estaires.	
Estaires	10/3/18		The Battalion were placed under orders to move at one hours notice ready to reinforce the Portuguese Division in the event of an enemy attack.	
"	11/3/18 12/3/18 13/3/18		Battalion found several working parties, & in consequence training could not be proceeded with to any great extent. Inter-Brigade Transport competitions were held on this date. This	

Army Form C. 2118.

Sheet 2

9th Bn The Kings (Liverpool Regt)

WAR DIARY
or
INTELLIGENCE SUMMARY.
(Erase heading not required.)

Instructions regarding War Diaries and Intelligence Summaries are contained in F. S. Regs., Part II. and the Staff Manual respectively. Title pages will be prepared in manuscript.

Place	Date	Hour	Summary of Events and Information	Remarks and references to Appendices
Estaires	14/5/16		Battalion were not quite as successful in their Competition as they usually are	
	15/5/16		The Battalion were deeply occupied in finding working parties. Inter Battalion competitions were held on this date. Competitions in wiring, musketry, platoon & company drill all took place as well	
			The Divl armd guns returned	
	16/5/16		During the period nothing unusual occurred. The Battalion were engaged in the usual tiring providing working parties	
	20/5/16		The Battalion relieved the 9th Bn Norfolk Regt in the trenches	
	21/5/16		of this day	
In the trenches			The situation during the day was quiet	
	22/5/16			
	23/5/16			
	24/5/16		Anzac day was observed to the extent that all leave was cancelled. All officers & ORs who on courses were ordered to rejoin their Unit. Schools having been closed. Numbers of men who had proceeded on leave Courses had not embarked returned to duty	

Army Form C. 2118.

WAR DIARY
or
INTELLIGENCE SUMMARY.
(Erase heading not required.)

Place	Date	Hour	Summary of Events and Information	Remarks and references to Appendices
In the Line	28/2/18		The situation during the period was very quiet. Scouts patrols sent out for the purpose of securing identification but was unsuccessful	
"	29/2/18		The situation during the day remained very quiet. At 8.30 pm a Raiding party went out for the purpose of securing identification. A shoulder strap belonging to a "Murtemberger" was found on a corpse in the enemy front line. Orf. handed to Brigade O/C. The raiders entered the enemy's front line trench found days deserted. All of the raiders returned to our line without suffering any casualties	
	30/2/18		Notification was received that the Battalion was being relieved on the night of the 30/31st inst. One strong Fighting Patrol went out tonight to secure identification. No enemy were seen and the patrol were unable to secure identification and returned to our line	
	31/2/18		The Battalion were relieved on the evening of the 31st by the 1st Bn. and proceeded to Huitrents en Artois	

J.P. Dow
Lieut Col
Comdg 9th Bn. [illegible]

57th Division.
172nd Infantry Brigade

9th BATTALION

THE KING'S LIVERPOOL REGIMENT

APRIL 1918

9th Bn. The Kings (Liverpool Regt.) T.F.

Army Form C. 2118.

WAR DIARY
INTELLIGENCE SUMMARY

(Erase heading not required.)

Instructions regarding War Diaries and Intelligence Summaries are contained in F. S. Regs., Part II. and the Staff Manual respectively. Title pages will be prepared in manuscript.

HEADQUARTERS
9th BN. THE KINGS
(LIVERPOOL REGT.) T.F.

Place	Date	Hour	Summary of Events and Information	Remarks and references to Appendices
ESTAIRES	1/4/15	10 a.m	Battalion relieved in Haubourdin Sector on 31/3/15 – 1/4/15 proceeded to Hubersart at Estaires. At 10 a.m. the Battalion proceeded to HAVERSKERQUE & arrived there at 4.0 p.m. The march discipline of the Battalion was very good.	
HAVERSKERQUE	2/4/15		During the morning kit & feet inspections were carried out by Company commanders. At 3.0 p.m. the Battalion proceeded to STEENBECQUE for entrainment. The entrainment was completed by 6.0 p.m.	
DOULLENS (at)	3/4/15		The Battalion detrained at 1.0 a.m. & proceeded to SUS-ST LEGER. The night was very dark & the roads were in a very bad condition. A few men fell out on the march, but on the whole the marching was very good. The Battalion arrived in billets at 6.0 a.m. The troops were rested during the morning, & during the afternoon further inspections were carried out.	
SUS-ST LEGER	4/4/15		The time was chiefly devoted to cleaning equipment &c.	
"	5/4/15		The Battalion proceeded to WARLUZEL, arriving there at 7.30 p.m.	
WARLUZEL	6/4/15		The usual programme of training was carried out during this period. On arrival at Warluzel a draft of 260 of Reserve	

2nd Sheet.   9th Br. The King's (Liverpool Regt) B.E.F.

Army Form C. 2118.

WAR DIARY
or
INTELLIGENCE SUMMARY.
(Erase heading not required.)

Instructions regarding War Diaries and Intelligence Summaries are contained in F.S. Regs., Part II. and the Staff Manual respectively. Title pages will be prepared in manuscript.

Place	Date	Hour	Summary of Events and Information	Remarks and references to Appendices
WARLUZEL	6/4/16		Joined the unit from England. The draft were chiefly composed of youths who had just attained the age of 19 years, who appeared to be very keen.	
"	8/4/16		The Battalion proceeded by route march to THIEVRES at 10.0 a.m. arriving at destination at 12.30 p.m. During the last hour of the march it rained very heavily. Consequently the troops were very wet. The afternoon was devoted to the drying of clothes, cleaning up of equipment, inspection of feet &c.	
THIEVRES	9/4/16		The usual programme of training was carried out, though not to the same extent as hitherto owing to lack of training grounds. Several very interesting reconnaissances on points to be manned in case of an attack was carried out during this period.	
"	11/4/16		Battalion proceeded by ROUTE MARCH to SOMBRIN. The marching to Sombrin was very bad, a large number men fell out.	
SOMBRIN	12/4/16		A large number of men who had fallen out on the previous days route march paraded for medical inspection. A large percentage	

C.P. Johnson
Capt.

Army Form C. 2118.

WAR DIARY
or
INTELLIGENCE SUMMARY.
(Erase heading not required.)

7th Bn. The King's (Liverpool Regiment) T.F.

Place	Date	Hour	Summary of Events and Information	Remarks and references to Appendices
SOMBRIN	13/4/15		of these men were marked "Duty" by the Medical Officer. Instructions were received from Brigade Head Quarters that all men so marked by the M.O. had to receive further training in route marching that afternoon. The route march was proposed owing to further orders being received for the Battalion to proceed to HENU. The Battalion left Sombrin at 10.30 p.m. The Battalion proceeded to BEAUCAMP Rd. arriving there at 12.30 am. The Battalion bivouacked for the night in the wood.	
BEAUCAMP Rd	14/4/15		Facilities for training were very poor at this place. During the afternoon the men who had fallen out on the line of march to Sombrin were taken for a few mile route march. In addition, men who did not feel up to the present standard of route marching were also taken on this march.	
HENU	15/4/15.		The Battalion moved into camp at HENU. The arrangements for training in the camp were found to be very satisfactory. The rifle range, in field reserving to this unit, was found	

Army Form C. 2118.

A⁴ Ghee 9ᵗʰ Bn. The Kings (Liverpool Regiment) 2.F.

WAR DIARY
or
INTELLIGENCE SUMMARY.

(Erase heading not required.)

Instructions regarding War Diaries and Intelligence
Summaries are contained in F. S. Regs., Part II.
and the Staff Manual respectively. Title pages
will be prepared in manuscript.

C.B.B...
Capt

Place	Date	Hour	Summary of Events and Information	Remarks and references to Appendices
HENU	[dates]		very useful for training purposes. Every alternate day during this period, the Battalion found working parties for work on points to be manned in case of enemy attacks. The work was carried out very successfully congratulations were received from the Divisional Commander. On the days the Battalion did not furnish working parties, field training was carried out. Several competitions took place on the rifle range which all concerned enjoyed great keenness. A competition between teams from Lewis Gun & Rifle Sec also took place. *proved very interesting. Prizes were given for this competition. The Lewis Gun teams company first secured prize in 1ˢᵗ Rifle team 2ⁿᵈ prize. The men who were not up to the present standard of route marching were taken on several route marches during this period. The effect of this has been very beneficial to the Battalion, the tendency to fall out on the line of march having decreased to a very appreciable extent.	[illegible marginal notes]

2353. Wt. W3541/1454. 700,000. 5/15. D.D.&L. A.D.S.S./Forms/C. 2118.

5th Sheet 9th Bn. The King's (Liverpool Regiment) T.F.

Army Form C. 2118.

WAR DIARY
or
INTELLIGENCE SUMMARY.
(Erase heading not required.)

Instructions regarding War Diaries and Intelligence
Summaries are contained in F.S. Regs., Part II.
and the Staff Manual respectively. Title pages
will be prepared in manuscript.

Place	Date	Hour	Summary of Events and Information	Remarks and references to Appendices
HENU	14/4/18		Several reconnaissances on foot to be made by the Battalion in event of defensive or offensive operations were carried out during this period.	
	21/4/18		The opportunities for Battalion sports were very good. Full advantage of by all the troops. The results on the whole appear to be exceptionally keen on keeping up the Battalion reputation for sports. Several very interesting competitions with divisional teams in the Div. took place.	
			On the 19/4/18, Major H. Hope D.S.O. Royal Lancaster Regt was appointed Acting Second in Command of the Battalion vice Major E.P.L. Rose who is to be attached R. Pott. m. Was very pleased to welcome Capts. H. Lawes and L. L. Brown who have returned to duty from England on 21/4/18. Col Beall reports to duty.	
	26/4/18			

F M Dow Lieut Colonel
Comdg 9 Bn The King's (Liverpool) Regt T.F.

Sheet No. I

9th Bn. The King's
(Lpool Regt.) B.E.F.

Army Form C. 2118.

WAR DIARY
or
INTELLIGENCE SUMMARY.

(Erase heading not required.)

Instructions regarding War Diaries and Intelligence
Summaries are contained in F. S. Regs., Part II.
and the Staff Manual respectively. Title pages
will be prepared in manuscript.

VOL 16

16.9

Place	Date	Hour	Summary of Events and Information	Remarks and references to Appendices
	MAY '15			
HENU	1		The weather was very dull. & the general was in a bad condition. A practice attack was carried out by A & D Companies. The remaining two Companies carried out the usual training & firing on the Range.	
"	2/3		Usual training was carried out on both these days.	
"	4		The Battalion was engaged in a practice attack and carried out in an exemplary manner. Every detail of the attack was carried out in an effective & successful manner, & the Commanding Officer received the congratulations of the Brigade Commander for the excellent manner in which the Battalion had done its work.	
"	5		The Battalion relieved the 1st Bn. Manchester Regt. in the Right Sub of the South Section (trenches). About 300 reinforcements arrived & were accommodated in the rear Battalion Head Quarters was established at a Sunqued Ridge Enuguere.	
Sanctuary 6/5 Wood			During the tour the entire garrison were employed on making & improving trenches, digging communication trenches & carrying and fatigue work. Reliefs were carried out by the 1st Bn. the Cameron High-	

Sheet No. 2

9th Bn The Kings
(Liverpool Regt) T.F.

Army Form C. 2118.

WAR DIARY
or
INTELLIGENCE SUMMARY.
(Erase heading not required.)

Place	Date	Hour	Summary of Events and Information	Remarks and references to Appendices
SOMMECOURT WOOD	11/13		Sommecourt Park was made into our impregnable & all round defensive position with a Central Keep.	
" "	13/13		Heavy Gas shelling took place, commencing at 7.30 pm. continuing until 9.45 pm. We sustained 24 casualties.	
" "	14		The Corps Commander, F Coys. inspected the defences constructed by this Unit in Sommecourt Wood, personally congratulated the Commanding Officer on the magnificent work the Battalion had done.	
IN THE LINE	14/15		The Battalion relieved the 1st Bn Royal Munster Fusiliers on the left sub sector. The Battalion was distributed in depth. D Coy on the front line. 'A' Coy in support. 'B' Coy in reserve. 'C' Coy Counter-Attack Company.	
" "	15		Situation quiet. 1 O.R. wounded & later died of wounds at Advanced Dressing Station. A reconnoitring patrol left our lines to observe enemy movement, but nothing unusual was noticed.	
" "	16/17		Situation continued quiet. 'C' Coy relieved 'D' Coy in the front line. The usual patrol left our lines but did not observe any unusual activity on the part of the enemy.	

D.D.&L.

Sheet No 3

9th Bn The Kings
(to good pages) 2 2

Army Form C. 2118.

WAR DIARY
or
INTELLIGENCE SUMMARY.
(Erase heading not required.)

Place	Date	Hour	Summary of Events and Information	Remarks and references to Appendices
IN THE LINE	MAY 17	15	Battalion HQ and mine shelters shelled from 7.20 am to 8.30 am. Two out of three of the mine entrances were blocked. The enemy obtaining 2 direct hits. 3 O.R. were wounded. During the remainder of the day the situation continued quiet.	
	18"		Situation continued quiet during the day. The usual patrols left our lines to observe enemy movement, but nothing unusual was reported.	
	18/19		B Coy relieved A Coy in the front line.	
	19		Lieut A.T. Barker left out a small daylight patrol across no MANS LAND. Before proceeding very far he suddenly encountered an enemy sentry. As this appeared to be a strong enemy post & the patrol was only 3 strong, the patrol leader decided at attempted to return to our own lines and report his discovery.	
	20/21		A fighting patrol of 19 O/R commanded by Lieut L. St Cochrane left our lines at midnight to engage the post discovered by Lieut Barker and to obtain information. They approached the post opened it heavily armed. They attempted to cut the wire surrounding same under the observation of the enemy in the post who numbered about 30, who	

WAR DIARY or INTELLIGENCE SUMMARY

Army Form C. 2118.

Sheet No 4. 9th Bn. The King's
(Liverpool Regt.) T.F.

Instructions regarding War Diaries and Intelligence Summaries are contained in F. S. Regs., Part II. and the Staff Manual respectively. Title pages will be prepared in manuscript.

Place	Date	Hour	Summary of Events and Information	Remarks and references to Appendices
	30/3/17		at once opened fire on them. The patrol replied & a sharp fight took place but owing to the strength of the wire it was found impossible to enter the post, & the patrol returned to our own lines. As far as could be ascertained seven casualties were inflicted upon the enemy. We sustained one slight casualty.	
	31		A small fighting patrol commanded by Lieut. Parkes left our lines at 12.10 am for the purpose of obtaining identification. They proceeded across NO MAN'S LAND to ROSSIGNOL WOOD & were not long before they engaged a small party of the enemy. Sharp fighting took place but the party were unable to obtain identification. We sustained one casualty.	
	1/4/17		During this period a great amount of salvage work was done with very satisfactory results. The material salved being employed at E.93 by Divisional staff.	
ROSSIGNOL FARM	2/4/17		The Battalion was relieved by 8th Bn. Yorks Regt. & Coys were accommodated at the Chateau at la Heure & 3 Coys & HQ Details were accommodated	

WAR DIARY or INTELLIGENCE SUMMARY

Army Form C. 2118.

Instructions regarding War Diaries and Intelligence Summaries are contained in F.S. Regs., Part II. and the Staff Manual respectively. Title pages will be prepared in manuscript.

(Erase heading not required.)

Place	Date	Hour	Summary of Events and Information	Remarks and references to Appendices
May 22/94.	22		Three days were spent in comparative tranquility. Calls burying parties were found at night. Burial was carried out by C Coy companies at RICHEBOURG FARM. Bn HQrs moved up to the Chateau de la Haie. Z=Col JHM Grew was being in need of a rest, Major So Kerr NC assumed command. While at the Chateau Bn HQrs had the pleasure of being closely associated with the HQrs of the 1st Bn R Munster Fusiliers, and it is interesting here to record that this was not the first time the Bn had the honour of working in conjunction with the illustrious Regt. Many members of the Bn could clearly remember how the 9th had the honour of relieving the 2nd R.M.F., elements of which were incorporated in the 1st R.M.F. after the battle of Ypres in 1915, in to 30 July use of the 14 Div. The Battalion relieved the 1st Bn R.M.F. in Keir trench where A+D Coys and the L Gunners of B were accommodated. B+C Coys remained in the Chateau de la Haie trench. This was heavy shelling of Aleys area during the evening but no casualties were sustained. The bank came tactically under its	
REE R. TRENCH	23			

WAR DIARY
or
INTELLIGENCE SUMMARY.
(Erase heading not required.)

Army Form C. 2118.

Instructions regarding War Diaries and Intelligence Summaries are contained in F. S. Regs., Part II. and the Staff Manual respectively. Title pages will be prepared in manuscript.

Place	Date	Hour	Summary of Events and Information	Remarks and references to Appendices
REER TR.	25.		Orders of the 170 Infy Bde while in Reer trenches. Gas Shells known as Yellow Cross Shells were fired over 'A' Coys Occlrs in the early morning. The men quickly adjusted their masks and no casualties were sustained. The rest of the day passed quietly.	
"	27.		These days were fairly quiet.	
RUM TRENCHES.	25/9		We Bn relieved the 2/7th L.N.L. Regt and occupied to reserve position in the left Bde sector. Bn HQ was Headquarters in Commercourt Wood with 2nd Q at the site of an old German incinerator enclosure. 'A' Coy was in the centre and 'C' Coy on the centre with Coys in support trench and 'D' Coy was on the left flank in Pigeon Wood. Coy 2nd in Comme with orders to inform a strong point, known as Julian Point in case of an attack. Obviously was afforded of studying the scenery of the enemy front on trenches, there fortified sentry boxes, observation posts, and the throughness of the mined dugouts, several of which were occupied by the [?].	
"	29/9		These days were spent in consolidation purposes. To Butler [?] several working parties.	
			There was abnormal sickness during the time in the trenches, due in all probability to the effects of gas.	

S[?]th Major
Comdy. 2/5th R. [?]

1st Sheet

9th Bn. The King's (Liverpool Regiment) 2.S.

Army Form C. 2118.

WAR DIARY
or
INTELLIGENCE SUMMARY.
(Erase heading not required.)

Place	Date	Hour	Summary of Events and Information	Remarks and references to Appendices
GOMMECOURT	1.6.15		The Battalion was in reserve to the Brigade in the left Brigade Sector at GOMMECOURT. with No.1 Quarter in the old German Support line north of Gommecourt Wood which was without Rum Support. "A" Company was disposed from right to left in the order B.A.C in Gommecourt Trench & Gommecourt Support. "D" Company was in reserve. The Companies were toured on usual duty by the enemy and again evidence of the activity of the Germans was seen in the usual reports received, sentry fires, subterranean movements & tells of an enlargement. At moving stand to the enemy put down a barrage on the German front. The S.O.S. went up at several places, our artillery - some of which was immediately opened up - opened with equal fire & transport told that the enemy used the night barrage casino without success. Who visited anything parties were Brigadier on the morning. The E. Corps Commander visited the Battalion Sector. The Battalion did considerable work in its own sector digging rifle steps & making duty of plant supports to become & repairs of the wire, the usual working parties. The day passed in comparative tranquility. Owing to the good works breaking of the parapet our observers were able to observe where dropped the enemy lines. Occasionally they could see some lookout of the enemy during shoot & sometimes horses grazing	An officer ladder & snipers rifle also a form of periscope seen which shape

Army Form C. 2118.

2nd Sheet

9th Bn. The King's (Liverpool Regiment) 27.

WAR DIARY
or
INTELLIGENCE SUMMARY.
(Erase heading not required.)

Instructions regarding War Diaries and Intelligence Summaries are contained in F.S. Regs., Part II. and the Staff Manual respectively. Title pages will be prepared in manuscript.

Place	Date	Hour	Summary of Events and Information	Remarks and references to Appendices
GOMMECOURT	5/6/18		The day was spent very quietly, there is nothing of interest to record.	
" "	5/6/18		The Brigadier commanding 190th Infantry Brigade visited the Battalion & inspected the organisation of the enemy line at Salmon Trench. Everything was very quiet in the evening & except portion of Salmon was seen. This day was also spent quietly.	
" "	6/6/18	5 am	The enemy opened a harassing fire on my Battalion Head Quarters with VII mm guns and 10.5 cm howitzers. The firing continued with frequent short intervals until 2 pm. The remainder of the day passed quietly.	
" "	7/6/18		The day was spent very quietly. There is nothing of any interest to state.	
" "	7/8/6/18		The Battalion relieved the 7th Bn South Lancs Regt in the left sector of the Left Brigade Front. Companies were disposed as follows:— "B" Coy Front Coy A — "C" Coy Coy D — Right Coy D — Relieved by 2 Battalion Head Quarters were established in Salmon Trench in the vicinity of a locality known as Salmon Point. The enemy engaged our front line recent activity. The Brigadier General visited the Battn.	
In the Line	9/6/18		Some rifle fire during the day. The enemy displayed the usual artillery activity. One enemy aeroplanes crashed over our lines & Halluskerts flew over the Battalion area at a low altitude for some time.	
" "	11/6/18		The day was fairly quiet. Our forward posts in front of Rossignol Wood were troubled by our own artillery which persistently fired short	

WAR DIARY or INTELLIGENCE SUMMARY

Army Form C. 2118.

3rd Sheet 9th Bn The King's (Liverpool Regiment) 28

Instructions regarding War Diaries and Intelligence Summaries are contained in F.S. Regs., Part II. and the Staff Manual respectively. Title pages will be prepared in manuscript.

(Erase heading not required.)

Place	Date	Hour	Summary of Events and Information	Remarks and references to Appendices
In the line	10.6.18		The enemy was noticeably quiet.	
"	13.6.18		The Duke of Marlborough & Hon Winston Churchill visited the Battalion sector accompanied by the Divisional Commander. The day was comparatively quiet.	
"	14.6.18		Artillery activity at night. The enemy occasionally commenced rifle & machine gun fire with an awkward angle from their front guns. The Battalion turned on many parties to assist the 3rd Corps trench Mortar & Lewis Gun Brigade Trench Mortar. The Brigadier General visited the sector. The batteries were relieved by the 3rd Corps Regiment 54th.	
	15.6.18		On relief the Battalion was disposed as follows. HQ Coys at the Château de la Haie + B & C Coys & Bn Headquarters at Roussel Farm. One Company from Rousselet Farm & one Company from the Château is to find working parties on the forward area at night. The sector remained very quiet during the day.	
ROSSIGNOL FARM CHÂTEAU DE LA HAIE	16.6.18			
	17/20.6.18		The sector proved very quiet. Working parties continued to work.	
	21.6.18		Working parties were found for work on new trenches west of the main A Battalion boxing tournament was held in the orchard at Rousselet Farm. All ranks evinced great interest. The various competitions lasted	

9th Bn The Kings (Liverpool Regiment) OF

Army Form C. 2118.

WAR DIARY
or
INTELLIGENCE SUMMARY.
(Erase heading not required.)

Instructions regarding War Diaries and Intelligence Summaries are contained in F. S. Regs., Part II. and the Staff Manual respectively. Title pages will be prepared in manuscript.

Place	Date	Hour	Summary of Events and Information	Remarks and references to Appendices
ROSSIGNOL FARM	21.6.18		A & D Companies moved from the Chateau-de-la-Haie & were accommodated with the remainder of the Battalion at Rossignol Farm.	
"	22/23	6.15	During the morning working parties were provided for the work on new trenches west of the farm. The afternoon was spent in general clearing up.	
In the Line	23/24	6.15	The Battalion relieved the 7th Bn Loyal North Lancs Regt on the right sector of the Right Brigade sector of the Tenth Divisional Front of the D. Corps. The trenches were found to be in a state of bad repair and steps were taken immediately to rectify this. A great amount of salvage was collected & sent over to the Salvage Dump. The Battalion found working parties as usual.	
"	24/25	6.15	This period passed very quietly. A short raid was carried out on Rossignol Wood, afterwards fighting patrols from the left Brigade penetrated into the wood. A number of casualties were inflicted on the enemy but no identification was obtained	
"	25.6.18		The situation continued to keep calm and there is nothing of note to report.	

5th Sheet

9th Bn "The King's" (Liverpool Regiment) 2.3

Army Form C. 2118.

WAR DIARY
or
INTELLIGENCE SUMMARY.
(Erase heading not required.)

Place	Date	Hour	Summary of Events and Information	Remarks and references to Appendices
In line	29.6.18.		Very quiet throughout the two days. The troops commander occupied the trenches on this day.	
	30.6.18.			

In the Field
30.6.18

S. [signature]
Lieut Colonel
Commanding 9th King's L'pool Regt.

Appendix A to
War Diary for the
Month June 1918

2nd Bn. The King's (Liverpool Regiment) B.E.F.

WAR DIARY
or
INTELLIGENCE SUMMARY.
(Erase heading not required.)

Army Form C. 2118.

Place	Date	Hour	Summary of Events and Information	Remarks and references to Appendices

A comparison of the strength of the Battalion at various times during the month is interesting. The strength on the various dates is shown hereunder.

	Eff. Strength	O.R.
1.6.18		959
8.6.18		931
15.6.18		903
22.6.18		880
29.6.18		888

The following Officers became non-effective:

Lt. Col. J.S. Le Brun, C.M.G. Inv. to Eng. sick 6/6/18
Lieut. J.O. Clement Inv. to Eng. wounded.
Lieut. J.W. Smith attached into 1st Bn. J.K's Exp. Force.

The following Officers were admitted to Hospital Sick:-
Lieut. B. Davenport dated 17/6/18
To A Eastwood 15/6/18
Lieut. A. Voyzey 14/6/18
Lieut. J. Hallett 25/6/18

During the month 1 Officer (Lt. A. R. Baxter) rejoined was accepted forwards and Capt. A. Hallett + 195 O.R. proceeded on 45 O.R. reinforcements joined.

The following Officers joined for duty during the month:-

Major J.H. Deering from 5th A.H.B. as temporary Second in Command
Captain J.H.B. Brooks
Lieut. H. Braedon
Lieut. K.J. Yates.

Halsall
Lieut. Colonel
Comdg. 2nd Bn. The King's (Liverpool Regt.)

Army Form C. 2118.

WAR DIARY
or
INTELLIGENCE SUMMARY.

(Erase heading not required.)

Army Form C. 2118.

Place	Date	Hour	Summary of Events and Information	Remarks and references to Appendices
"LINE".	1/2		The 8th of the Batt. on the line (GOMMECOURT SECTOR) and owing to a thaw and the situation still remained very quiet.	
AUTHIE.	2/3		The Battalion was relieved in the line by the 3/10th N.Z. Rifle Brigade and moved to again man AUTHIE and were encamped under canvas. The Battalion then became troops in G.H.Q. reserve.	
	4th		On arrival H.Q. and Battalion Headquarters reconnoitred the country including the RED LINE and PURPLE LINE. The remainder of the Battalion were engaged in general cleaning up &c.	
	5th 6th		The Battalion practised the manning of the RED LINE under Brigade Supervision. The morning was devoted to general training. A fact that was impressed throughout the &c &c during the afternoon the total weight of balls collected being 12 lbs 5oz².	
	7th		The being Sunday Divine Service was held. Afternoon to take was allotted to the Battn.	
	8/9		During the next two days Company training was carried out. Representatives from each Coy also took musketry in the PURPLE LINE during the ten days.	
	10th		Lefr Infantry working parties on the PURPLE RESERVE LINE. The work consisted of digging and also wiring the line in front of same. A fly circus was	
	11th		also carried out general training. A day consisting of attack on a strong-point, in the training ground at IGA.	18.9

WAR DIARY
or
INTELLIGENCE SUMMARY.

Army Form C. 2118.

Place	Date	Hour	Summary of Events and Information	Remarks and references to Appendices
AUTHIE	July 11		During the afternoon the Regimental Sports were held and a very good show was put forward. An open air Concert who was also going in the evening but, unfortunately the arrangement brought to an end by small cessation owing to the inclement weather.	
	12		Corps carried out general training while Bob boys carried out a tactical exercise and authorized scheme at I.8w.P.O.	
	13		B.C. Coys carried out general training and touring while the N.C.O.S attended at the Musketry School carrying advances, Kent and an out post scheme including advances, Kent and rearguards, at I.9w.a. output.	
	14		Today being Sunday Divine Service was held afterwards the Bde Sports were held — Great interest was manifested by all ranks. The Bn did very well at the Sports obtaining — 1 First prize. 8 Second prizes and the third prize. The usual general training was carried out by the Bn my having forward at I.8b.P.O.	
	15		The Little Raugh at I.8d was allotted to Bay today. It remainders of the Bn. Carried out the usual programme of training at I.15.a+c.	
	17		The Bn again attached a tactical scheme what consists of a surprise attack on a line thereof at T.19.20. w.o. Coys at a time practices this and when not engaged as the	

WAR DIARY
INTELLIGENCE SUMMARY

Army Form C. 2118.

Place	Date	Hour	Summary of Events and Information	Remarks and references to Appendices
AUTHIE	April 1917			
	18th		Scheme they carried out general training on training ground at I.9.a. Major (B.S. Read (?)) LORD McGREGOR Staff Reader Sgts. Worked jointly as Commanding Officer.	
	19th		The same training as on the 17th was again carried out.	
	20th		The Platoon of each Coy fired in the ARR Eliminating Competition. the Range at I.9.d. The remainder of the Bn carried out usual training on ground at I.9.a	
	21st		The Bn. again carried out tactical scheme for attacking "Enemy" across open country – Assault "Enemy" being four Coys. establishing. Defensive W carried along track I.16.D. an attack enemy position I.24.C.D.	
	22nd		Aeroplane type was h/a. Attempt made to hive buns were held and enemy numbers procured.	
			The Bn took part in an attack to think (enemy) to be held by the enemy along VAUCHELLES-AUTHIE road. The Bn. assembled for this attack in the reserve slope I.21.a.b.c.– I.19.a.b.c. to. Allowing the big shoots were told, this being attended by large numbers from troops.	
	23rd		The Inter-Platoon Competition in connection with the ARR Eliminating Competition was held on the range at I.9.a. Owing to very bad weather no further training was carried out.	

WAR DIARY or INTELLIGENCE SUMMARY

Army Form C. 2118.

Place	Date	Hour	Summary of Events and Information	Remarks and references to Appendices
AUTHIE	July 24th		4 P.M. C/R. Platoon fired M.G. to decide which Platoon's representatives to fire in the R.B. Distinguishing Competition. The firing were therefore represented to the winners and therefore deputed the firing in the Butt Competition. The platoon had in the R.B. scheme, consisting of practice in the attack on enemy trenches along VAUCHELLES – AUTHIE road. On deployment in the service slope at 1200 to – 1390 to 60 feet. Platoons were chosen by all units during the scheme.	
	26th		B Coy were allotted range at 180 and C Coy carried out General training in ground at 18a, 18c. A&D Coy carried on a Musketry competition today by 9 points. A M.G. platoon won the Butt eliminated.	
	27th		Bn Tactical scheme was to be carried out but owing to the inclement weather this was cancelled until Tuesday the 31st.	
	28th		Brigade Church Service was held on Boston Sands Grounds.	
	29th		7 this dropped to cleaning up etc. Baths were from camp at AUTHIE to billets at MARLUZEL followed a route PAS, GRINCOURT, COUTURELLE arriving at billets at 3.0 pm.	
	30th		Battn marched from MARLUZEL at 6.15 am. to ASHEULES SUIVANT. Transport camp attached by 4 hours.	

Army Form C. 2118.

WAR DIARY
or
INTELLIGENCE SUMMARY.

Army 9th Bn The King's (Pwee Regt) 7F

Place	Date	Hour	Summary of Events and Information	Remarks and references to Appendices
ARRAS	31st		Battalion moved at 8.30 to ARRAS preparatory to going into the line in Brigade reserve. The move was complete about 1.30 a.m. on the 1/6/17, the Battalion being billeted in Cellars &c in ARRAS. During this month the knee allotment greatly increased.	

H Stephens
Lieut Colonel
Comdg 9th Bn The King's (Pwee Regt) 7F

Appendix "A"
to War Diary
for July 1918

9th Bn The King's (Liverpool Regt) T.F.

Army Form C. 2118.

WAR DIARY
or
INTELLIGENCE SUMMARY.
(Erase heading not required.)

Place	Date	Hour	Summary of Events and Information	Remarks and references to Appendices

The following is a comparison of the strength of the Battalion at various times during the month

5/7/18	Effective Strength O.R.	908
12/7/18	"	910
19/7/18	"	912
26/7/18	"	975
31/7/18	"	953

The following Officers became non-effective:-

Lieut J.M. Vogan } Sick to
" H. Davenport M.C. } England
Capt J. Wright att. H.Q. 57 Div. proceeded on a Course to Aldershot
Hon't J. Lunt rev to Eng.
Capt R.J. Rider M.C. on
Lieut H.C.H. Ellis M.C. were to already granted whilst on Leave in England proceeded not to return

The following Officers were posted for duty.

Lieut. Col. Long DSO Seymour DSO Barraclough Simmons reported for duty on 14/7/18 as Commanding Officer

W G Simons
Lieut. Colonel
Commanding 9th Bn The King's (Liverpool Regt) T.F.

Army Form C. 2118.

WAR DIARY
or
INTELLIGENCE SUMMARY.
(Erase heading not required.)

Army Form C. 2118.

Place	Date	Hour	Summary of Events and Information	Remarks and references to Appendices
ARRAS	1st		Various inspections were held during 10 days while in ARRAS, under Coy arrangements. At 5.30 pm orders were received that the Battalion would proceed to WAKEFIELD and COLLINWOOD CAMPS A.26.d.15.15. Re Battn moved at 9.50 pm and arrived in camp at 11.15 pm. 3 Coys & H.Qrs were accommodated in WAKEFIELD camp and one Coy (A) in COLLINWOOD Camp.	SHEET 51.b.N.W.
	2nd		Usual coy inspections of Arms Gas and the usual inspections were held during the day.	
	3rd		Two Coys were on the range and 2 Coys would march. Coy Cmdrs proceeded to reconnoitre assembly positions for peace Zone in the event of an enemy attack.	
	4th		Two being the 5th Anniversary of the declaration of War in voluntary church was held in COLLINWOOD CAMP A.26.c.1.2. No few from each Coy attended. A voluntary service was also held in B to commence at 6.30 pm.	SHEET 51.b.N.W.
	5th		Two Coys carried out a route march and 2 Coys carried out forrest handling in vicinity of CABLU. Various exercises also held. The Battn carried out a reconnaissance assembly positions. During the afternoon ST CATHERINE and ANZIN were occupied to the B. "A" & "B" Coys "A" & "B" Coys, 3VC & 3rd Plat Coys carried forrest smiths were placed and "A" & "D" Coys formed.	
	6th		One Coy was on the alerted HG, and one Coy were on the rge. HG & L.G. section during the day in the HG Section HG of L.G. helped playing equipment in the one in H.G. & 3 The Comon forestation of furnished lectures to the 57 N.C.O's. Balm were again allotted to the men. No 120 men. The first 6—	

19.2

Army Form C. 2118.

WAR DIARY
or
INTELLIGENCE SUMMARY.
(Erase heading not required.)

Instructions regarding War Diaries and Intelligence Summaries are contained in F.S. Regs., Part II. and the Staff Manual respectively. Title pages will be prepared in manuscript.

Place	Date	Hour	Summary of Events and Information	Remarks and references to Appendices
ARRAS	6th		Inter-Coy football matches took place this afternoon. B & D. Coys found working parties. The Batn found a working party of 100 diggers for work on CHANTECLER SWITCH from H.1.d. 60.38 to H.8.b. 10.90.	SHEET 51 b NW.
	8th		The Bn again found working parties, strength of same being 100 for work as above.	"
	9th		The Bn relieved the 1st RMF in the left sub section of the left Brigade Front, FAMPOUX NORTH SECTOR.	
	10th		The usual duties were carried out in the line. The following casualties were sustained:—	
	11th		Lieut. J. Gardiner + 1 O.R. Killed	
	12		2 O.Rs. Killed and 2 O.Rs. Wounded	
			1 O.R. Killed	
	13th		Bn Headquarters and trench mortars moved to POINT DU JOUR at H.30.60.90.	SHEET 51 b NW.
	14th		The usual duties were carried out in the line. During this tour in the line the trenches/line and it was exceptionally quiet, except at night when the wound hostile TMs were carried out by both the enemy & ourselves.	
	15th			
	16th			SHEET 51 b NW
			In the return of the 16th, a discharge of gas projectors was carried out just south of the GAVRELLE ROAD in H5. Held who practically no retaliation.	
	17th		The Bn was relieved in the front line by the 1st/3rd Black Watch. After relief the Bn proceeded to ANZIN where they assembled breakfast, arriving at 14-45 a.m.	
	18th		Afterwards at 6.0 am the Bn entrained on the Light Railway and proceeded to CHELERS where they detrained and marched into billets in BAILLEUL and CORNAILLES arriving there about 10-15 a.m. After dinner the day was devoted to REM and in the evening the usual inspections were carried out.	
	19th		Today was spent in cleaning up, taking of returns &c.	
	20th		"A" Coy carried out a tactical scheme in conjunction with the 1st RMF. 3 Officers	

Army Form C. 2118.

WAR DIARY
or
INTELLIGENCE SUMMARY. (Erase heading not required.)

Instructions regarding War Diaries and Intelligence Summaries are contained in F. S. Regs., Part II. and the Staff Manual respectively. Title pages will be prepared in manuscript.

9th Bn. Lethergh Regt (Major ?)

Place	Date	Hour	Summary of Events and Information	Remarks and references to Appendices
BAILLEUL	20th		and 3 ROs per Coy attended. Two Officers reports for duty — 2/Lt Oliver and 2/Lt Wheen.	
	21st		The Batln. was allotted this unit at TINQUES. The Batln. proceeded by Route March, at about 10:15 a.m. from BAILLEUL-aux-CORNAILLES to FOSSEUX, arriving in billets about 3.15 p.m. immediately on arrival billets were served, afterwards the Batln. being reset till 1 p.m. when dinners were served.	
FOSSEUX	22nd		The Bn. received orders to proceed again to BOIS GUERMAISON arriving in billets at 6.15 a.m. Breakfast were again (except dinners) immediately on arrival. the Bn. again rested until (dinner teas served at 1 p.m. Rifle inspections was also held) afterwards.	
BOUQUE-MAISON	23rd		The Bn. received orders to proceed to BARLY, arriving in billets about 3.15 a.m. Breakfasts were served on arrival. afterwards there was a period of three Hours. no troops of movement b/tween then and the (crossroads?) The Bn. remained in billets in Barly (orders) as usual.	
BARLY	24th		The Bn. received orders to be prepared to move at 10 a.m. However it was 1 p.m. when the Bn. left for SAULCOURT. Only (train?) was traveling into Saulty was crossed the Bn. entered (?) During ever long on BARLY during ___.	

D. D. & L., London, E.C.
(A500) Wt W7771/M2039 750,000 5/17 Sch. 52 Forms/C2118/14

WAR DIARY or INTELLIGENCE SUMMARY

Army Form C. 2118.

9th Bn (?) (Loyal Regt)

Place	Date	Hour	Summary of Events and Information	Remarks and references to Appendices
BELLACOURT	26th		Further orders. During the day the Battn was equipped with Bombs, Rifle Grenades etc, ready for proceeding into Battle. All men's packs etc, were stacked at Regt. Stores. At 11.0 pm the Battn paraded & moved via FICHEUX, BLAIRVILLE, to vicinity of MERCATEL where sky bivouaced.	
HENIN.	27th		The Battn rested during the day until 5.pm. The Battn paraded in Fighting order at 6.pm & proceeded to vicinity of HENIN, where sky has tea at about 6.pm. At 9.30.pm the Battn moved forward to the HINDENBURG LINE & took over trenches in V.7.c. relieving a Battn of 52nd Division. The relieving was completed by 4.am. Occupation of trenches was completed by 4.am. Verbal orders were received at 6.am on the 28th inst. that the Battn would attack during the day. At 9.am Bn. H.Q. was established at BLOCK HOUSE at T.6.d.5.3 and afterwards moved forward to U.7.c.9.6. While moving & assembling were received from Brigade detailing the Battn to attack the following Objectives. Zero hour to be at 12.30.pm. the Battn. Btn on the RIGHT First Objective. U.15.c. Central - HOOP LANE - to junction of CROSS TRENCH with HOOP LANE. Second Objective - RIENCOURT.	
HUMBER-court	28th			

WAR DIARY
or
INTELLIGENCE SUMMARY.
(Erase heading not required.)

Army Form C. 2118.

[unit:] 9th Bn. York Regt.

Place	Date	Hour	Summary of Events and Information	Remarks and references to Appendices
HUMBER REDOUBT.	28th		Bn. Operation Orders were issued at 10.5 am. Coy. & the orders by 11.30 am. Had warning orders not been received from Brigade early in the morning, it would have been impossible to have got into position to commence the attack at 12.30 pm. The own Bn. Battle was:- D Coy - Right Front. C Coy - Left Front. A Coy - Support B Coy - Reserve The 2y/K.S.L. Regt. on the Left. - First Objective HENDICOURT. The 1st Q.W. Rifles on the Right. - Final Objective BULLECOURT. The Companies advanced as under:- D & C Coys - Along S.E. edge of HUMBER TR. 2 Platoons of each Coy, and mop up as leading Coys advanced. A Coy - In rear along HUNNER TR. Platoons & Maclean. B Coy - 2 Platoons on Main Road in U 4 a 3.7 & 47.6.74 2 Platoons in SENBURGH LANE. B Coy were responsible for dealing with rear of M.G's which were in U.T.C.	

Army Form C. 2118.

WAR DIARY
or
INTELLIGENCE SUMMARY.
(Erase heading not required.)

9th Bn. The Wilts. R — 1 Bose Regt

Instructions regarding War Diaries and Intelligence Summaries are contained in F. S. Regs., Part II. and the Staff Manual respectively. Title pages will be prepared in manuscript.

Place	Date	Hour	Summary of Events and Information	Remarks and references to Appendices
HUMBER-R REDOUBT	28th		Coys. parties assembly Complete Synchronised watches at 12.10 pm at 12.15 pm the Barrage for the Right Bn Camerons opened — there was slight retaliation on our trench. At 12.30 pm. our barrage opened, the Batln. commenced to move forward. The jump was not too good owing to the wire. numerous shell holes. Shortly after Zero, the contact Aeroplane received a direct hit by a shell. This being rather an unfortunate incident on the eve of the attack. "B" Coy came into contact with enemy M.G. along SUNKEN ROAD in U.8.c. but these were very effectively dealt with & No. 36 Grenade barrage and these prisoners togethr with 1 M.G. were taken. Very heavy fire was directed against the leading Coys both from the vicinity of COPSE TRENCH and also from RIGHT REAR, formations in vicinity of U.13.b. After advancing about 500 yards the leading troops came under our own barrage, but owing to troops on both flanks continuing beyond its path, this pushed on. Several Casualties occurred in Consequence. An enemy M.G. in U.13.b. became very	

Army Form C. 2118.

WAR DIARY
or
INTELLIGENCE SUMMARY.
(Erase heading not required.)

(1st Bn R[oya]l [illegible] Reg[imen]t)

Place	Date	Hour	Summary of Events and Information	Remarks and references to Appendices
FOG ALLEY etc.	29.4		Troublesome as troops were advancing on FOG ALLEY. Two enemy M.Gs + crews were taken prisoner on reaching FOG ALLEY. Several Outpost in COPSE TRENCH were dealt with by throwing bombs down. Men in pairs of the enemy and Nicoli sniper being to escape. Three [illegible] M.G.s were also captured in the vicinity and its crew either taken prisoner or killed. From the ponds [?] to the final objective very little resistance was encountered. [illegible] on reaching the first objective A's & B's Co[mpanie]s followed up the leading Co[mpanie]s. The PoW up as they went forward. At about 1.50 p.m. the FOG ALLEY - Batt[alio]n captured the advance from the Heavy M.G. fire was encountered from the direction of HANSCOURT ALLEY in U.16.b. Major Bomphy together with about 10 men and Capt[ure]d a M.G. also capturing Nickey the [illegible]. when in front of SPANISH ALLEY in U.16.b. a considerable amount of gas was encountered and several Canister [?] revealed. The enemy also put up shells just in vicinity of CRIX and COPSE TRENCHES in U.16.b and a. and U.5.b and d.	

WAR DIARY or INTELLIGENCE SUMMARY

Army Form C. 2118.

Place: L/pool Regt.
Date: 26/4

Two parties of about 15 men each under a Sergeant advanced on the S. of HENDICOURT, took some prisoners together with three light M.G's but as they got mixed up with the Stokes Coy side slipped out beyond D. Coy.

At about U.10.c. a strong point was encountered, most of the enemy were killed, and 3 M.G's were captured. A little further on Major BOWRING was killed.

A party under 2/Lieut C. STENT. advanced into the village of HENDICOURT and were met by enemy M.G. fire; a burst on their front ruined houses. Lieut Williams B. Officer 2nd/4th C, and 2/Lieut Marwell "A", came along with some parties and scouts. He Coy reported there were now 4 our troops on either side of the village. It was therefore decided to withdraw to CEMATERY AVENUE, and hereto up U.10.c and a while withdrawing Lieut WILLIAMS and 2/Lieut DALE became casualties.

WAR DIARY
or
INTELLIGENCE SUMMARY.
(Erase heading not required.)

Army Form C. 2118.

9th R.Ir.Rif (Pioneer Regt.) 77

Place	Date	Hour	Summary of Events and Information	Remarks and references to Appendices
	25th		One Company of the enemy were seen forming up in U.5.e to Counter-attack, but they were dispersed by M.G. and L.G. fire. Afts re-organization the following were the dispositions:-	
			1. Q.2.S.R. - 2 Officers and about 30 O.Rs. together with 30 Officers and about 15 O.Rs of the 2nd S.L.R. in vicinity of CEMETERY AVENUE, U.10.d.50.60.	
			Lieut. C.G.R. HILL. - 2 Officers and about 130 O.Rs holding a front U.10.d.50.63. and CEMETERY TRENCH in rear and Serpent-Luis in trench U.10.d.30.50.	
			One Officer and 30 O.Rs of the 1 R. Brigade forms a strong Point and defensive flank in vicinity of U.16.b. Central.	
			No touch was obtained with any troops on either flank of the above dispositions, but it was known that a few Canadian M.Gunners together with a small party of the Baston and 6.S.W. M.CARTIN were established at the Junction of ULSTER AVENUE with ULSTER TRENCH.	

WAR DIARY or INTELLIGENCE SUMMARY

Army Form C. 2118.

9th R.B. Rif. the Kings 1st/7 R.R.

Place	Date	Hour	Summary of Events and Information	Remarks and references to Appendices
	25th		which the above parts were in the village, an attempt was made by a portion of D'Coy, to advance round the N. side of the village, but they were held up by heavy M.G. fire from CROWS NEST and from trenches in U.16. central. A Stray Point of about U.10.d.9.0.70 was captured by the party above, and 8 prisoners taken. Owing to the very heavy M.G. fire which was coming from the direction of CROW'S NEST, and the fact that the left flank of the Bn. was in the air, and an enemy Artillery shelling the village, it was decided to withdraw to trench in U.10.d. Consolidate there, and hold on. 2/Lieut STENT went back into the village after withdrawal and informed the party of the 1st Q.V.R. North Bn was on our right in CEMETERY TRENCH. This party then withdrew to CEMETERY TRENCH. Others were at Shirley after 4 pm. and own as the consolidated line. 2/Lieut FAXNER proceeded to find Bn. H.Q. and succeeded in doing so at 4.30 p.m. Between 4.30 p.m. & 6 p.m. a head	

WAR DIARY or INTELLIGENCE SUMMARY

Army Form C. 2118.

Place: 9th Yorks (W. Regt)
(1 Dose Regt)

Date	Hour	Summary of Events and Information	Remarks
25/9		9. "A" Coy under Capt. McCARTEN came up out of the Valley in U.2.c. and were advancing on HENDECOURT. This party was met with heavy M.G. fire from SUNKEN ROAD in U.4.b.c. 50.70. The party then advanced under the command of the C.O. (Lieut-Col. Lord J.G. Seymour) by short rushes to ULSTER TRENCH near junction of ULSTER AVENUE with this trench, where a line was established, and the party of "A" Coy, placed under the command of J. Canadian R.G. officer, who also had several men and a few M.G's at this point. They were in addition 60-70 above about 15 to 20 O.R. of the 2nd S. & R. at this point. This position was very heavily shelled and Trench Mortared, the Comdg. Officer (Lieut-Colonel Lord J.G. Seymour D.S.O.) being wounded at the junction of ULSTER TRENCH with ULSTER AVENUE, at about 4 p.m. A second Bn. H.Q. were afterwards established at U.9.a. 50.10 where they remained until 6.11 a.m. on the 29th.	

WAR DIARY or INTELLIGENCE SUMMARY

Army Form C. 2118.

(Royal Regt.)

Place	Date	Hour	Summary of Events and Information	Remarks and references to Appendices
	28th		From 4 am to dusk, the positions occupied by the unit were heavily shelled by own 18 Pounders, and also every 8" and 5.9". The Batt. suffers numerous casualties in consequence. The above disposition were held until 10:30 am on the morning of the 29th inst, when orders were received by Bn. H.Qrs. to withdraw to COPSE TRENCH owing to 10th Brigade advancing at 1 P.M. Companies D & 2/4th L.N. Lancs. moved up and occupied its trenches which were being vacated by this unit. Battn. H.Qrs. moved forward from HUMBER REDOUBT at 1.30 P.M. on 28th. Advance under very heavy M.G. fire from trench on J.13.b sustaining severe casualties. Advanced Bn. H.Qrs. was established at about 3 pm in shell hole in U.9.a.60.10. The Commdg. Officer, Lieut: Colonel Lord H.C. Seymour D.S.O., the Adjutant Capt. W. Rain M.C., then went forward to ascertain the situation. While doing this a platoon	

WAR DIARY
or
INTELLIGENCE SUMMARY.
(Erase heading not required.)

Army Form C. 2118.

Place	Date	Hour	Summary of Events and Information	Remarks and references to Appendices
G.H.Q. Line Trenches (Appx "A")	28th		Many attempts were made to effect communication with Brigade H.Q. owing to casualties to Battn runners during the advance, these were not successful. Capt. D. Raine M.C. assumed command of the Battn at 5 pm on the evening of the 28th inst. The Bn. suffered fairly heavy casualties during its attack, particulars as below. 12 Officers 231 Other ranks. Lieut-Colonel Lord H.G. Seymour DSO. Major F.W. Bowring Capt. J.A. Main Lieut. A.S. Nash M.C. " D.A. Dickson " E.V. Thompson " T.G. Jones " A. Naylor " W.B. Briggs " H.M. Wilcox " G.H. Dale Officers	Rounded Killed Wounded 85 ? ? ? 8 8 2 ? 8	

WAR DIARY or INTELLIGENCE SUMMARY

Army Form C. 2118.

1st Bn L'pool Regt.

Place	Date	Hour	Summary of Events and Information	Remarks and references to Appendices
	28th		The following moon's information was received at about 9.30am that 75th Brigade was going to attack at 1pm. It was therefore decided to withdraw the Batn. to CORSE TRENCH. This was completed by 12/15 pm. the 110th Brigade attacking at 1pm. At 11am on 29th inst, Major B.C. Baillie (Royal Munster Fusiliers), assumed command of the Battn. from then onwards.	
	6 29th			
	30th 31st		The Battn. moved out of CORSE TRENCH on the afternoon and returned to Bivouac area in HENIN. Evening this about 6pm on the evening of the 29th when dinners were served to the men. The Battn. H.Q.(Offices) on a 2 Company Basis during the 30th & 31st & 1st day of the month.	

WAR DIARY
or
INTELLIGENCE SUMMARY.

G.H. Bn R. Fus(?)

Loos Rgt.

Place	Date	Hour	Summary of Events and Information	Remarks and references to Appendices

The following identifications were obtained:-

103rd Regt.   58th Division.
11th Coy, 132nd I.R.   39th Division
180th I.R.   26th Reserve Division
121st I.R.   26th Reserve Division

The Battalion captured:-

1. Trench Mortar at U.9.c.10.15.
19. Prisoners.
14. Machine Guns.

Tues. 3.9.1918.

[signed]
Major Commanding
9th Bn The R(?) Fus Regt

WAR DIARY
INTELLIGENCE SUMMARY
(Erase heading not required.)

Army Form C. 2118.

9 Liverpool R.
1/7/[?]

20.G

Place	Date	Hour	Summary of Events and Information	Remarks and references to Appendices
HENIN	2/9/18		O.i/c. The Range (Liverpool Regt) The Bn moved from Boisseux Area, Henin at 4:15 pm to trenches in vicinity of FRENER'S LANE. Bn HQrs being established at T6a. 30.45. move being completed by 7:50 pm. Lieut. H. Darling the party of guides left HQrs at 6:30 pm for forward position; as this party was passing through FONTAINE they were dispersed by shell fire resulting in loss of 9 ORs (1 Lieut. S. Wounded). Lieut. Darling reported incident returned to rendezvous at 10:50 pm. East of the Bn moved forward to positions at 8:30 pm arriving at 4:45 am on morning of [?]. East just enough time to occupy positions before our barrage commenced at 5 am for 172nd safely Brigade attack. The 172nd Brigade attack was quite successful all objectives being reported taken. My 1st Bn Royal Fusiliers & 11th Essex on right resistance was encountered by the 10th Lanc. Regt on right. At 7 am the 63rd (Naval) Division moved up for the attack which passed through our trenches. All objectives were taken, & very little opposition was encountered by them. The enemy were seen scurrying over the numerous ridges in this undulating Sector, and our artillery, Horse & Motor transport moved up with the consistent advancing troops	
HENDECOURT FRENCH	2/9/18			

WAR DIARY or INTELLIGENCE SUMMARY

Army Form C. 2118.

Place	Date	Hour	Summary of Events and Information	Remarks and references to Appendices
HENDECOURT TRENCH	29/9/18		9 Bn. N. Rifle Brigade. Telephone communication between Coys & Bn. H.Qrs was successfully accomplished. During the afternoon the enemy heavily shelled vicinity of Bn. H.Qrs with 5.9's. 77's. Casualties 1 O.R. wounded 1 O.R. killed. Lieut. T.W. KNEEN became a casualty during the afternoon. During the morning a patrol was sent out to reconnoitre OPELING WOOD with a view to silencing enemy machine gun, reports being returns. On reaching the objective no men fatal to be one of our own. The party was commanded by Lieut. J.M. PARKES. No enemy were found in the vicinity. "Y" Coy under Capt. ROADS. DSO.MC was sent forward & occupied trenches in U.19.a.y.b. at 12 noon. "X" Coy under Capt. E.J.G. ROBERTS. MC. was sent forward & occupied trenches in U.2.d.b. at 4 pm. The enemy continued to shell Bn. H.Qrs. vicinity during the evening.	
	30/9/18		Orders were received from Brigade for the Bn. to march to trenches in U.13.a.+ d. (in vicinity of TUNNEL TRENCH) The Bn moved off at 3.30pm., & proceeded via KEND ROAD	

WAR DIARY or INTELLIGENCE SUMMARY

Army Form C. 2118.

Unit: 9th Bn. N. Staff. Regt.

Place	Date	Hour	Summary of Events and Information	Remarks and references to Appendices
FONTAINE-CROISILLES Road to new area	30/8/18		Bn was ordered to move to new area. On arrival (4.0 pm) dinner was served. Rest of the day being devoted to erecting shelters & bivouacs	
	1/9/18 6th		From the 4th to the 6th the Battalion re-organised. On the 6th the Bn received warning orders from Brigade that the Bn would relieve the 18th Inf. Brigade in support on the 7th Sept. Orders were received from Brigade that the Bn would move on 7th Sept. Relieve the Royal Irish Regt. of the 16th Inf. Brigade.	
	7/9/18		The Battn moved off from area V.13.a.00.30 (Army) at 11.00 am Route - Ressemont, Ruyaulcourt, Cagnicourt. "B" "C" "D" Companies were taken at Transport lines where the Companies by Capt. Kay (Qmr) Dinner was served on route. (Lieutenant) Marks being served at 2 pm. At 2.30 pm Bn continued advance and the Bn was passed through Ribecourt. Capt. D. Rain M.O. being seriously wounded, he was evacuated to the Fd Ambulance. The Battn reached the R.O.R. relief being completed at 7.10 pm Bn HQrs established at 25.a.50.30. Lieut C.B. Green reports from transport lines to assume the duties of Adjutant.	Op Oaks H.No.1

WAR DIARY
or
INTELLIGENCE SUMMARY.

(Erase heading not required.)

Army Form C. 2118.

Place	Date	Hour	Summary of Events and Information	Remarks and references to Appendices
MPON	7/9/18		The situation was somewhat quiet on our front; except for hostile shelling of Battern during period from 7p.m. night to 6 a.m. 8/9/18, about 50 short new Dugouts across Rockerrie in vicinity of Y. Coy. No hostile Camp reports.	
	8/9/18		A reconnaissance party composed of Major Buel M.C., Capt. Roberts, L. Watling M.C., Lt. Burns W.S.R.R., H.C., & Lieut. Young left 32 HQ a at 10/45 am to reconnoitre forward area & lines of approach to INCHY EN ARTOIS, in event of the Battn being called upon to deliver a counter attack in two eventuality. Party left orders at Battn HQ. in V.26.a.o.o. & then proceeded via Hindenburg Support Line to Battn HQ o of 17th K.R.R. in Dugouts at A.4.d.30. From this point the party reconnoitred BUSSY SWITCH on D.6.d. and proceeded from the latter S.E. to INCHY. The party returned to Battn HQ via INCHY - CROISCOURT Road, arriving at Bnt. HQ. about 4pm. At 7p.m. "G" "H" Hostile Howitzers were firing V.2.5.T. Shrapnel batteries in V.25.t. Howbers had third Guns were firing and a heavy later gas T.B. from V.25.a.7.4. This was immediately reported to Brigade by runner.	

WAR DIARY or INTELLIGENCE SUMMARY

Army Form C. 2118.

Place	Date	Hour	Summary of Events and Information	Remarks and references to Appendices
Q Bn. The King's Own R.R.	9/9/15		Lieut. Nalwig A.C. took a party, consisting of 3 Offrs & 4 N.C.Os to reconnoitre position manned by E.O. on 8th inst. C.O. acted as by Battle H.Q. to attend conference with G.O.C. Division.	
	10/9/15		The Battn. relieved the S. Lancs Regt. B.H.Q. moved from V.26.a.y and Bat. aver H.Q. from 9th S.L.R. in HINDENBURG SUPPORT at D.U.A.6.U. "B" Coy. moved into position in trench S.4.A. "C" Coy. in D.S.C. "A" Coy. relieved D Coy of 9th S.L.R. in BUSSY SNITCH in S.6.d. "D" Coy. relieved A Coy of 9th S.L.R. in S.6.b. relief being complete by 10 p.m.	
	11/9/15		Information was received at 9 p.m. that the 171st Bde. Royal would attack advance positions of enemy N. of CANAL on E.2 - E.5 - E.14 Major Bass R.E. received instructions from 171 Bde party to reconnoitre WARCBURG TRENCH from E.13.a.7.8. to where it joins CAMBR - du - NORD - NORMAN STREET from E.13.6.3.2. across CAMBR & up to QUARRY WOOD. Also where HINDENBURG SUPPORT runs into MAUVRES Major Bull Inc. 9th Lieut. Dailing A.C. and scouts via South of INCHY through HINDENBURG SUPPORT & S.A.Q. of 218th K.L.R. head to O.P. at E.13.6.3. when a good view was obtained of ground to be reconnd. They returned to B.H.Q. D.U.A.6.U. at 11/45 pm. B.H.Q. was fixed for 6.15 pm.	

WAR DIARY
or
INTELLIGENCE SUMMARY.

Army Form C. 2118.

Place	Date	Hour	Summary of Events and Information	Remarks and references to Appendices
9 Bn The Argyll & Suth'ld Highrs	11/9/18		At 6/15 am Batteries on Right of Corps Front opened fire putting down smoke barrage S.W. of BOURLON WOOD, Barrage was kept up, and 3 minutes after woods were shelled. At 6/15 pm batteries on Corps front opened with shrapnel H.E. on Enemy trenches West of CANAL, E.2. E.E. Etc. Creeping barrage up Coys. Enemy fired many S.O.S. signals but only feeble reply from his Artillery. Our infantry attacked. No information received regarding Operations until 8 am 11/9/18, when summary drew confirmed that our attack had failed a.m.s. Right Batt. got forward & established with Guards Brigade Third G.M. of MOEUVRES. Left Batt. was held up by M.G. fire, severe casualties & without their Skirting parties, the Casualties being fairly heavy. The enemy kept up harassing fire during & to hours of darkness on the whole front Right 9,500 yards. Hostile Aeroplane flew over our lines at 10 pm. Light Sig. Shelling dropped to North in vicinity of INCHY. N.E. of FROMVILLE at 9.30 pm. At noon orders were received to prepare for lifting Orders - Major Jack 7/9 Cameroonians Bg. Comdr to be	

WAR DIARY or INTELLIGENCE SUMMARY

Army Form C. 2118.

Place	Date	Hour	Summary of Events and Information	Remarks and references to Appendices
	11/9/18		Conference at Bat. H. Qrs. at 8.30 p.m.	
	12/9/18		At 4 am orders were received to move forward then two Coys in support, then two Coys in reserve. B & C Coy in support — Bn H.Q. was established at Bloch House Trench D.6.c. 6/8. B Coy moved into position in HINDENBURG SUPPORT from S.12.a 60 to S.12.a 97, and C Coy in HINDENBURG SUPPORT – D.6.c. The Batn. relieved 2/4th K.R.R. with Left Sector during night. A Coy took up position in front line on the left of the Batn. astride F.1.h.2.6. D Coy left up position in right sector of Batn. area in GRANDCOURT Rd at E.1.d.9.7. D Coy took up position at D.b.d. in BUSSY SWITCH - WINDERBURG SUPPORT. E Coy were established at VAULX H Qrs as Counter attack Coy. Batn H.Qrs was established in SUNKEN ROAD at D.6.c 60.10. Relief was complete at 9.45 pm. The night was very quiet.	
	13/9/18		The enemy shelled ZACHY very heavily during the afternoon & night. Barrages were called at BOIS H.Q. afternoon. A Coy was relieved during night by C Coy. There was delayed by enemy shelling, this only one casualty was reported. 2/Lieut. J. Rohult went out on a Coy with a patrol of	

WAR DIARY
INTELLIGENCE SUMMARY

Army Form C. 2118.

Place	Date	Hour	Summary of Events and Information	Remarks and references to Appendices
	15/9/18		9th Bn. The Manchester Regt. "A" Coy relieved "B" Coy in left front sector during the evening. Relief being completed at 10:30 pm.	
	16/9/18		Enemy towels removed by Capt. B.B.G at about 10 am accompanied by the Intelligence Off. & No. 1 & 2 to reconnoitre both fronts. No enemy other Officers were seen. Returned about having met a spoke day light patrol during the tour. Their bodies were brought in by O.C of this Bn. Strength of patrol 9 O.R's (3 O.R's. & 1 2/Lieutenant & 3 O.Ranks of this Bn.)	
BULLECOURT	17th		On the night 16/17th the Bn. was relieved, proceeded to Brigade area at Bullecourt by 16 H.L.I, this about 11 am. About 2 am attempts were made to construct some improvised bivouacs which were very unpleasant as they arrived at the Brigade area.	
	18/9/18		On the 18th the Bn. proceeded by Route March from Billeting Area at Bullecourt arriving they about 2pm. The remainder of the day was devoted to rest.	
BAILLEULMONT	19/9/18		On the 19th Coys were placed at the disposal of Coy Comdrs for thorough inspection etc	

WAR DIARY or INTELLIGENCE SUMMARY

Army Form C. 2118.

Place: Bloemen(?)
Prepared by: Lt. (signature)

Date	Hour	Summary of Events and Information	Remarks
13/9/18		1 N.C.O. & 2 men were proceeding towards the Camps, when an enemy M.G. opened fire on them. A/Cpl. R____ was hit. The Sergt. slightly wounded. Enemy shelled vicinity of Bn. H.Qrs. and range at intervals during night. The Corps Commander (Sir Charles Fergusson) visited Bn. H.Qr. about 11/15 p.m. Divisional Commander visited Bn. H.Q. about 2 p.m. C.O. & Company Commander of the 16 Highland Light Infantry visited Bn. H.Q. during afternoon to reconnoitre prior to relieving the Battn.	
		Lieut. Pauling M.C. went out on Patrol at 10 p.m. to locate enemy M.G. Our Light Trench Mortars were notified to fire 30 rounds on the post at 5 a.m. next morning. Enemy Shelling during the day was normal, both areas were only slightly shelled. 1 N.C.O. (Segt Johnson) was killed by M.G. fire.	
14/9/18		Enemy shelled morupres and T7J Park Copse heavily from 5 a.m. to 6 a.m. Infy was also shelled. Some gas shells. The Brigadier called at Bn. H.Q. at 9.30am. Liaison lost with 76 G.O. Advanced parties of the 64 N.F. I arrived during the	

WAR DIARY
or
INTELLIGENCE SUMMARY.
(Erase heading not required.)

Army Form C. 2118.

O.C. 1/4 Kings (Liverpool Regt.)

Place	Date	Hour	Summary of Events and Information	Remarks and references to Appendices
LAGNICOURT	27/11/17	9 P.M.	The Kings (Lpool Regt.) road, arrived at new area about 6 p.m. Supplied General Coy. to E.39 R.0.6.6 on temporary proceeded to Reception Camp. BOIELLES Bombs, flares etc were drawn and distributed to them. During the day the Battalion was warned to prepare for Action.	
	29/11/17		At 1.30 a.m. the Battalion moved from Bivouack area to positions of assembly in the HINDENBURG LINE.	
	30/11/17		At 1.10 a.m. the Battn. Joined on behind HQ for to took followed them along track as per allotted route. The going was very bad on account of mud and heavy rain. The Battn arrived at place of assembly in HINDENBURG LINE D.16.a.65.40 to D.17.a.05. at 3.40 p.m.	
		5 A.M.	The Commanding Officer Liaison Officer reported at Divisional HQ to for final conference. Battalion moved forward at 3.30 A.M. following HQ Bn. 7th K.L.R. Progress slow under getting out into the open beyond TADPOLE COPSE, passed through MOEUVRES and crossed CANAL DU NORD at 8.30 A.M. Continued advance towards S.W. corner of BOURLON WOOD at 9.15 A.M. got into artillery formation. Occasional shells and bullets were held up from 9.15 to 9.45 when advance was through. Enemy Aircraft overhead firing on troops. Heavier than five m.G. from the M.G.B. again held up, then advance continued + Battalion	

WAR DIARY or INTELLIGENCE SUMMARY

Army Form C. 2118.

Unit: 9th Bn. The King's (Liverpool) Regt.

Place	Date	Hour	Summary of Events and Information	Remarks and references to Appendices
BAILLEULMONT	20/9/18		The Battn. utilized the Rifle Range & 2 Coys carried out Tactical scheme.	
"	21/9/18		The Battn. carried out Training on the following lines:- Gun Drill - Musketry and Drill etc.	
"	22/9/18		This being Tuesday, Divine Service for the Battn. took place. In the afternoon the Brigadier Genl. presented the recipients of the Military Medal who had been gained during the action on 29th August, with the Ribbon.	
"	23/9/18		The Battn., with the exception of Lewis Gunners, Rifle Grenadiers & men carrying out a Tattoo Scheme, proceeded to the Range, & carried out firing practices. The Battn. dined at 1 p.m. & carried out Tattoo Scheme as in plan to previous day. On the evening of this date the Battn. received warning Orders that the Brigade resumed move from present area to VRAUCOURT by train, on 25th inst.	
"	25/9/18		The Battn., and Transport Echelon, paraded at 10 a.m. & marched to BEAUMETZ Station, entraining at 12 noon & detraining at VRAUX VRAUCOURT at 5 p.m. The Battn. then proceeded by route march to Bivouac area at LAGNICOURT which preceded ...	

WAR DIARY or INTELLIGENCE SUMMARY

Army Form C. 2118.

Place	Date	Hour	Summary of Events and Information	Remarks and references to Appendices
Bourlon	Sept 28		9 A.M. The Reving. Infantry Regt. Getting over the crest came under heavy Machine Gun & M.G. fire. Pressed on and got going into position NE of ANNEUX and SW corner of BOURLON WOOD going through the My H.M.G. We suffered many casualties. The Commanding Officer found the C.O. of the R.M.L.I. and got information that the 2nd Division had not taken ANNEUX. The R.M.L.I. were rather scattered and only one party of 15 had been located at all. At 3 p.m. a message was sent down on GRAMCOURT and ANNEUX and these places were taken. The enemy were seen retiring behind ANNEUX and country south. The Commanding Officer saw the C.O. of 75 Canadian Battalion who was moving forward from N to S of BOURLON WOOD on to FONTAINE and received the following his boys. Going the southern part and then to endeavour to capture CANTAING TRENCH. This was held up on account of receiving instructions from the Infantry Brigade that a Barrage was being put down on the trenches. No troops were therefore further withdrawn as no hill top Hy M.G. fire attempt was made at 6.30 but was held up by M.G. fire from the trenches and a coy of N.Z. from Return in BOURLON WOOD. Capt. G.F. Buchel and Lieut. T.W. McKimmon and four other ranks were wounded. The Battn. withdrew & took up position in trench	

Army Form C. 2118.

WAR DIARY
or
INTELLIGENCE SUMMARY.
(Erase heading not required.)

Signed: C B Ames Lt Col

Place	Date	Hour	Summary of Events and Information	Remarks and references to Appendices
Bourlon Wood	Sept 28		1st Bn the Kings (L'pool Regt.)	

ANNEUX and BOURLON WOOD.

From arrival throughout the day & night the whole area was subjected to intermittent bursts of gun fire after the taking of ANNEUX and BRAINCOURT it eased off considerably, but until this occurred the fire was very hot also from M.G. after dark the line was readjusted and the men dug themselves in.

The following were in action:—

Major Sir Ball S.B. Commanding Officer. Lieut Col Johnson Adjt.
Lieut N Kerr, Signalling Officer. Lieut H.J. Willets Intelligence Officer.
2/Lieut Knock ass'tt Scouts. 2/Lieut E.E. Kemp Lewis with Section.

A Coy Lt A Roe. M.C. (OC) Lieut Sponge, 2/Lieut Wilkinson.
B Coy Lt J.H. Young (OC) 2/Lieut L Lutterworth, 2/Lt H. McLean.
C Coy Capt G J Buckle (OC) 2/Lieut Van Rugby, Lieut C.B. Hunt.
D Coy Capt J Atkinson (OC) 2/Lieut S.H. Hill, 2/Lieut Wyatt.

9 X.Ops. Other Ranks.

The casualties sustained during the day and night were:—
Capt G J Buckle, Lieut C.B. Hunt, 2/Lieut J.H. Young, 2/Lt J.H. Wilkinson wounded and other ranks
9 Killed
40 Wounded
2 Missing

Army Form C. 2118.

WAR DIARY
or
INTELLIGENCE SUMMARY.
(Erase heading not required.)

9th Bn. The Kings (L'pool Regt.) 13

Place	Date	Hour	Summary of Events and Information	Remarks and references to Appendices
ANNEUX	28/9/18		At 5.30am the Battalion received orders to withdraw to the Transport lines 1½ miles behind ANNEUX but later to proceed down the CANTAING LINE and occupy trenches in about F.26 Central. The night was spent here.	
	29/9/18		Quiet day in same location. Overhaul of stores & equipment, deficiencies & replaced and men given a restful day. The Commanding Officer attended Brigade & received particulars of operation for the following day.	
	30/9/18		The Battalion paraded at 2.30 am and moved off at 3.00 am as follows:-	
			Major McBall MC Lead to B Johnson Lt Lt Legs Lt Kreule	
			A Coy Lieut Roe MC Lieut Sparge 2nd Lt. 61 O'Keefe	
			B Coy 2/Lt Butterworth 2/Lt Nelson 2/Lt Howe 75 "	
			C Coy 2/Lt. Rigby 2/Lieut Heywood & 78 "	
			D ___ Capt J Atkinson 2/Lt McHill MC 2/Lt Wyatt 95 "	
			B.H.Q 77	
			top 9	
			2/Lieut Challoner & Lieut Luro 2/Lt L.S Ned & 1 Section No 2 of 54 M Coy marched off with Battalion.	

Army Form C. 2118.

WAR DIARY
or
INTELLIGENCE SUMMARY.
(Erase heading not required.)

Instructions regarding War Diaries and Intelligence Summaries are contained in F. S. Regs., Part II. and the Staff Manual respectively. Title pages will be prepared in manuscript.

Place	Date	Hour	Summary of Events and Information	Remarks and references to Appendices
S of CAMBRAI	30/9/18		2nd Bn. The Kings (Liverpool Regt.) 1/3 Battalion reached Canal trough at 5.30 a.m. prompt. Troops who had been sent ahead at 5.10 a.m. to reconnoitre reported the Battalion at 5.35 a.m. Arrived at junction of roads all in touch where the 16 Manchr. Iws were to be met at 5.30 but at 5.30 as the latter Battalion had not arrived by 5.30 and it was getting light the Commanding Officer decided to get the Battalion out into artillery formation at once without waiting any longer for them & this was done. The R.H.Q. began to arrive at 5.35 and were passed through forward. During this time Hanky Lenny etc the two Coys concerned and immediate at got tight and typing all the troopers in position a barrage was put down on the assembly position and the M.G. fire increased.	
		6.30 a.m.	The Battalion was assembled by 6 a.m. Coys began to move forward via following the R.H.Q.	
		7.0 a.m.	B.H.Q. followed up at 7.0 a.m.	
		8.4.M	B.H.Q. followed up with "D" Coy and found what Battalion held up by heavy shelling in Battalion area before to breakdown all to M.G.	1
		9 a.m.	Lieut. Reade reported Battalion entirely held up in conjunction with R.H.Q. on ridge in N.D.R.	
		9 p.m.	Disposed of and Mops to find gunners and endeavour to get held up by M.G. battery.	

D. D. & L., London, E.C. (A8011) Wt. W1771/M2031 750,000 5/17 Sch. 52 Forms/C.2118/14

WAR DIARY or INTELLIGENCE SUMMARY

Army Form C. 2118.

Place	Date	Hour	Summary of Events and Information	Remarks and references to Appendices
S. of CAMBRAI	30/9/18	7.30am	9th Bn. The Buffs (April Regt.) (5) Lieut Sleep returned and reported Major Atkinson forward with R.M.O.	
		7.30am	Lieut Sneade with Lewis patrol went forward to get further news of situation. No 5 fire mainly from PROVILLE district and over fire from the right. 5.9 high trajectory shot 10.2 mainly from direction of front and right. Suffering many casualties.	
		?	Sent small patrol forward to find Medical Officer and staff, who has failed to report at 50/16.	
		7.50am	Sent small patrol out to locate HQ of Bn. 2.	
		8.25am	Lieut Snead returned from his reconnaissance. Senior Company somewhere mixed. A.C. D located (60 men) at A 76 a. 7. to A 76 c. 96. Remainder from Senior Road in A 25 d. 60 90. to PARIS COPSE. Held up by M.G. fire from Tunnel and Flesho enemy occupying trenches from A 19 central to A 20 d. and A 20 d. 60 ye and so. Germans informed Gerfritz were spotted at A 20 d. lot Germans informed	
		9am	R.M.O. visible only on line from A 26 a 2 ½ to A 25 d. 50 95. 3rd to Engineers carrying trenches from A 19 central to A20 d. Seogn. Co at carrying lunder cover of this to get forward. Medical officer not having arrived sent out a search party to end woods to find him.	

Place	Date	Hour	Summary of Events and Information	Remarks and references to Appendices
S. of CAMBRAI	27/8/14	9 am	9 Am the Hemp (Alford Regt) L.I. Not having seen anything of O.S. Lot. sent Ihout Keep scout party to locate S.L.R. and report in touch.	O.S.I
		9.53	Hemp Road returned from his 2nd reconnaissance forward and reports that the 2 right forward Coys. had been unable to get forward, that effort of our battling fire or trenches in front opposed to have [?]. That the enemy a little. He could obtain no news of [?] — 7 M.F. His Coys. being reorganized to push forward to right and try to reach 2nd Battn. on our right still held up. M.G. fire still heavy. R. Munster Fusiliers not got gone ahead. Shelly showed for awhile, but is now [?] heavier again.	
		9.8 am	Ithound Keep J.T. on return with O.S. St. who we are now carrying forward behind no. 9. The Company Commander of [?] he spoke was unable to inform him when BHQ. was. He was given location of ours.	
		11am 11/6am	Brigade Orderly troops still held up. No further progress forward. O.C. reports that part of his "C" Coy. and E. to Coys were still unable to get further forward, that left flank of "B" [?] on his right were equally held up, that certain trenches to front had gone ahead of him on early [?] of morning and to his right, in an easterly direction. He believed they had been told up and could not get further forward. He was instructed to send out patrol in touch with them, and obtain news of situation as regards trenches [?] [?] trouble beyond.	

WAR DIARY

Army Form W.3118

Summary of Events and Information

Place	Date	Hour	Summary of Events and Information	Remarks and references to Appendices
CAMBRAI	30/9/18	11.20 am	R.A.P. Established near Bn. H.Q. being shelled and M.G. firing	
		11.30 am	Sent to Brigade for more Stretcher Bearers.	
		11.50 am	Second patrol which had been sent out to find R.H.Q. returned and reported Location of their Bn. H.Q.	
			Sent Lieut Cheale to obtain & bring back information.	
			2/Lieut Kerr than as Liaison	
		12.3 pm	Instructions re fresh attack (B.M.357) received and acknowledged. Commanding Officer sent for Company Commanders and explained to them the new attack to be made at 1 pm	
		1 pm	Barrage put down and later smoke perched up. Lieut J. moved forward to make original objective. This was not successful as they were held up by heavy M.G. fire and enemy aeroplane about 100 yards. This Battalion being now contingent only on the R.H.Q. being successful, a further advance was not made, and situation report sent in.	
			Commanding Officer spent afternoon visiting coys and keeping with R.H.Q. and S.R.M.	
			Endeavoured to get message through to Brigade but was broken	
		3.30 pm	Sent report on situation by runner	

Army Form W.3118.

WAR DIARY

of 1st Bn the Kings (Liverpool Regt)

Place	Date	Hour	Summary of Events and Information	Remarks and references to Appendices
	3/4/18	4 pm	Got through on phone to Brigade and spoke to Brigade Major on Situation. A little later the Brigadier Reconnoitring Officer visited H.Q of ANSON Bttn and got information as to situation at PRONVILLE and trenches in N.E.N.S.	
		5 pm	Commanding Officer went to join 2 I.C. to meet the Brigadier	
		6 pm	Commanding Officer went to Companies and reorganised positions	
		8 pm	Instructions received that Battalion would hold position during night seem back to trenches E. of FONTAINE	

Signed
Lieut-Colonel
Comg 1st Bn The Kings (Liverpool Regt)

Army Form C. 2118.

WAR DIARY
or
INTELLIGENCE SUMMARY.
(Erase heading not required.)

Instructions regarding War Diaries and Intelligence Summaries are contained in F. S. Regs., Part II. and the Staff Manual respectively. Title pages will be prepared in manuscript.

21.G.

Place	Date	Hour	Summary of Events and Information	Remarks and references to Appendices
Cambrai	1/10/18		Battalion moved from positions on the open slopes of Cambrai at 2.30 A.M. to West side of LA FOLIE WOOD. No shells or aeroplanes being very wet night stood about until daylight. On arrival men were issued with porridge & tea-rum. In daylight trees were lopped & men got clothes dried as well as possible. Shelters were dug & men got to sleep after breakfast. Remainder of day spent in getting bivouacs & digging shelters. 6 O'Comp 3 O.R's 10 O'C companies met. Camel Back & Trenches up to MARCOING LINE where we were ordered to hold in First Army Counter attack. HQ established in wood. Slight shelling of area.	
La Folie Wood Fontaine	2/10/18		Whole battalion in area East of Fontaine & Rear of La Bois ... engaged all day getting ... felt to positions. 8.50 moved up the morning air cold. Quiet no one being wounded by mine (one died). Enemy aircraft over at night. Somewhat ... noise. Capt Atkinson being wounded & sent back to wounded.	
	3/10/18		Men employed on Lewis Gun practise & Palmey. No incident throughout day & night. Our own aircraft were over.	

Army Form C. 2118.

WAR DIARY
or
INTELLIGENCE SUMMARY.
(Erase heading not required.)

Instructions regarding War Diaries and Intelligence Summaries are contained in F. S. Regs., Part II. and the Staff Manual respectively. Title pages will be prepared in manuscript.

Place	Date	Hour	Summary of Events and Information	Remarks and references to Appendices
LA FOLIE WOOD DISTRICT CAMBRAI	3/10/17		but no casualties. Very cold at night. Enemy attempt bombard district at night. Many casualties in S. Lancs who were alongside the Nord.	
	4/10/17		Slight shelling in A.M. 11 A.M. wood being shelled. 1 killed at entrance of dugout. W.R. hitting two prisoners. 2/Lt. Krabbe sent away to the Transport lines sick & I/Hull came up to take over no work on intelligence offrs. About 2 P.M. the Brigadier & Brigade Major were both wounded by a shell which came through entrance to the dug out & exploded in room. Both wounded in the head & face serious. Colonel Vaillance (Seaforths) took on acting Brigadier & Major McKergo Own R.A.R. 2nd Brigade. Orders received & Relief Kilwergo Own R.A.R. in PROVILLE. Relief carried out in early evening quite successfully.	
PROVILLE	5/10/17		During night & early morning fair amount of shelling of Ridge & Coy's in front dug in. Remainder in houses not forward. "D" Coy & "A" Coy in trenches on S. side with 1 Coy 5 ? Monsters ? about. Brigadier came round had C.O. in the morning and without ... of the position. Very little shelling during day, but good deal of M.T. Mortars on C. Coys ?	

WAR DIARY
or
INTELLIGENCE SUMMARY.

Army Form C. 2118.

(Erase heading not required.)

Place	Date	Hour	Summary of Events and Information	Remarks and references to Appendices
PROVILLE	6/10/18		Granville & 2/Lt Hood shelled intermittently during day. 2/Lt French wounded on the forward pass. One fell on a Clergy post killing 5 men. About 4.30 Ration party from B.H.Q. front Coys was caught by shell fire. Four men being wounded. B.G.C 171 Bde & CRE 57 K Divn both wounded by the same shell. Late in evening had orders that we were to be relieved by 2/7 KLR.	
SW of CAMBRAI	7/10/18		Battalion relieved by 2/7 KLR & 2r proceeded to A 25 c+d Cois about 2500 x S.W. of CAMBRAI & took over Support position from the 7th R.W.L. Fairly quiet night. Enemy Aby gas mean improved fire positions & Coy & Bn areas & carried Brigadier Genl round sector. Two Coys in Campbrai improving B Coy mind & fired positions forward & protection rifles manned First generation of Release ne collected & moved into dumps.	
	8/10/18		Any quiet during day but occasionally shelling round area at night. 3 men of D Coy 1 NCO. (1 killed 2 wounded) 1 man of H.Q. hit by M.G. bullet. 5 lances & R.M.O. straightened out their line emerging up on the right in conjunction with the 170 Bde who pushed forward & occupied position facing Mont in A 36 - A H a forming a defensive flank	

WAR DIARY or INTELLIGENCE SUMMARY

Army Form C. 2118.

(Erase heading not required.)

Instructions regarding War Diaries and Intelligence Summaries are contained in F. S. Regs., Part II. and the Staff Manual respectively. Title pages will be prepared in manuscript.

Place	Date	Hour	Summary of Events and Information	Remarks and references to Appendices
S.W. of CAMBRAI	8/10/18		The 63rd Divn at same time pushing through in East direction to objective E. of NIERGNIES – at objective new Coy Commanders preparing to reorgany when Notes of tanks not Coy Commander reported to Coy Hqrs. During night slight shelling. Two coys moving to Cambrai.	
	9/10/18		Enemy evacuated Cambrai during night. Early morning Bn. 173 Bn passed put down to Cambrai. Who attacked Troisville & passed through. Again at 5.15 enemy Bn 24th Div when attacked though at 5 A.M. H. 170 Inf Bde & 63rd Div. They had 5 squadrons the right of LE CATEAU. Canadian patrols in Cambrai early in morning. Able R.M.F. Sunes had patrols into the town also 170 Bde. We were engaged in salvage & burying dead. 2/ NELSONS & 7 others (killed in M.H. 30 & Copse) were later found & buried near PARIS COPSE	
		6 p.m.	Received orders that battalion would much through the night to BERTRY S. of FONTAINE. Moved out at 8.30. On arrival there found bivouacs & second instructions. Do got leave to proceed to our old area in the CONTAING Trenches – Arrived in at 1 A.M.	

WAR DIARY
or
INTELLIGENCE SUMMARY.
(Erase heading not required.)

Army Form C. 2118.

Place	Date	Hour	Summary of Events and Information	Remarks and references to Appendices
CANTAING TRENCHES ANNEUX	10/10		Quiet day spent here. Bugles called at 10.30. Men quite comfortable & happy.	
"	11/10		Orders received to move late in day. Marched out at 3PM. Went to MIRAUMONT – Sgt INCHY + W. of BOURSIES. Bivouacked a 15 Brigade sheet.	
NEW INCHY	12/10		Marched off at 2.15 to place of entraining East of HERMIES. The train to men did not ready for them on arrival & alarm fairly. Train 2 hours late. Trucks only. Travelled all night. Very cold.	
DOUVRIN	13/10		Arrived at Bethune at 10AM. Marched off to DOUVRIN. Breakfast on arrival. Running & cold. Men in huts & billets fairly good. Breakfast called at 2.30 + breakfast news that no more trains.	
"	14/10		Received marching orders in early morning. Battalion paraded & marched off at 8.20 AM. Embussed at VAUDRICOURT. Proceeded via Bethune Vieille Chapelle to Pt du HEM (1/2 mile SE of LAVANTIE) – after debussing Battalion moved forward by road. Arrived at 12.15 via Sgt LAVANTIE – FROMELLES to le MAISNIL. Took over from the 21st London as Regt-Reserve in support – the four companies are as trenches were. Headquarters at L of L	

WAR DIARY
or
INTELLIGENCE SUMMARY.

(Erase heading not required.)

Army Form C. 2118.

Place	Date	Hour	Summary of Events and Information	Remarks and references to Appendices
LE MAISNIL	14/10/18		HQrs at CARTER FARM. Enemy still holding line of Railway about 2500 X East. Quiet night. Division now in the 5th Army (General Birdwood) 11th Corps (Lt Gen Haking)	
"	15/10/18		In preparation for battle, relieving the 17th Manch - Regt from 8 Bn of 141 Brigade. CO, 2O + 4 Coy 3 OC succeeded to RADINGHEM at 9.30 AM. On arrival had news that enemy had retired from Aubers on our front + also on right. Patrols sent to ESCOBECQUES. Arrived on right established touch with SANTES. John reports our relief postponed 24 hours. Received further orders from Brigade meanwhile had called + given adjutant particulars regarding the positions + Brigade picketing LILLE. Mus City cleared. Quiet night. Fired HV shells in vicinity of C Company but no damage. Weather hot + heavy.	
"	16/10	10.30 AM	Received instructions to Stand fast but prepared to move forward at half hours notice. Had conference with Company Commanders at 9.30 + discuss advance on LILLE + picketing the City. The movement at LE MAISNIL has day on S. Lawes about forward to the Railway. B.H. pushed to RADINGHEM. 142 Bde advance continued on our front in conjunction with 59th Div (Left) + 74th Div (Right). Held up at HAUBOURDIN by MG fire. CO attended conference at 4.30 at Bde HQ at RADINGHEM regarding advance + picketing LILLE. Heavy damp weather. Rain.	

Army Form C. 2118.

WAR DIARY
or
INTELLIGENCE SUMMARY.
(Erase heading not required.)

Place	Date	Hour	Summary of Events and Information	Remarks and references to Appendices
LE MAISNIL	17/10/14	12.25 PM	Received orders to advance. Battalion assembled at 1.15 & moved off to HELLENES. BHQ & VERTBALLOT then proceeded joined Coys. News being received on the way (2.55 PM) from Bn.Hdqrs that the RM? reported all country ahead & canal round LILLE all clear of enemy. Battalion pushed on & arrived at canal at 4.55 PM. Bn. Int. Off. increased escort & ascertained that batteries really patrolled the outskirts of the city. An Indego had been Battalion from various of outskirts of the City. An Indego had been blown up, but the one at PONT CANTELEU was just at the crossing to single file. The canal was was very dense & the batterier was held in its getting across. Companies proceeded to their various areas. ? picquets were posted guarding all crossings over canal from CANON D'OR on the NORTH to PONTE D'ARRAS on the SOUTH. All men in position by 7.30 PM. & reports on state of bridges made & Sgt. Bn. Brigadier by 9.30. All bridges over the canal were blown up & Sig. PONT DE LA POSTE North of where could with more or less difficulty be crossed on foot.	
LILLE			Battalion H.Q. established in the AVENUE DE DUNKIRQUE was a chateau which had been occupied by the enemy. This no many others had been beautifully damaged & ? rifles rapidly wantonly destroyed before leaving. One enemy armed motorcar was taken at PONT BETHUNE. It had been hiding. No one killed on our side. Collected a few ? by RM H. Corps without a ?	

Army Form C. 2118.

WAR DIARY
or
INTELLIGENCE SUMMARY.
(Erase heading not required.)

Instructions regarding War Diaries and Intelligence Summaries are contained in F. S. Regs., Part II. and the Staff Manual respectively. Title pages will be prepared in manuscript.

Place	Date	Hour	Summary of Events and Information	Remarks and references to Appendices
LILLE	18/10/17		People had a very busy time trying to make the people not realizing they could not go to & from the City. Many were in great difficulty go through living outside they had been in the habit of going in & obtain keys & dress rations. All pickets will find us not while adjacent. General Moccer toured the City at 7.30 AM.	
		9.30 PM	C.O. put for A Brigade to arrange to find it frown & Anglesleham etc who was working the City following morning.	
	19/10		Guard of honour under Lt. Sowen Paraded at 8 AM 2nd & Rigby + Whymark + 100 Other ranks. Guard accompanied by Band of 4th S. Lancs in Position at PONT DE CANTELEU at 8.45 AM. M. CLEMENCEAU arrived at 9 AM - he inspected his Guard. Appreciation of the guard. The divisional Commander congratulated the C.O. on the excellent turnout of Guard. After the guard met their leader had marched through the City where it took up position opposite the Mayors House & waited after M. Clemenceau departure him. Great enthusiasm in the City mail was fully decorated with flags. B.C. Comp'y played a football match ag. 2/4 on the Bolletie ground.	

D. D. & L., London. E.C.
(A/o1). Wt. W1771/M2031 750,000 5/17 Sch. 52 Forms/C2118/14

WAR DIARY or INTELLIGENCE SUMMARY

Army Form C. 2118.

Place	Date	Hour	Summary of Events and Information	Remarks and references to Appendices
LILLE	20/10/18	4.30	Men not actually on private employed on preparing for General's order that we proceed forward towards ASCQ. Lanes to take over all pickets from us tonight. Bus was due commencing at 11 P.M. & finishing at 3.30 A.M. all reported relieved.	
LILLE ASCQ.	21/10	7.30 PM	Battalion (less A Coy 3) landed & passed starting point PONT CANTELEU at 7.45. Marched through LILLE A Coy 3 joining on at PONT DE LA POSTES. Fell misty & rainy. Proceeded through HELLEMES to ASCQ arriving at 10.15. the PONT LOUIS XIV. All billeted into very good billets. Inhabitants most obliging. Borrowed tubs & heated water. Whole battalion was bathed in the afternoon & clothes aired.	
ASCQ WILLEMS	22/10	10.15 AM	Brigade ordered to move into WILLEMS AREA. Passed starting point at 10.15 AM. Route - CHERENG, SIN. Battalion billeted in LA BREULE (Bmk) & TREQUIERE (Belgium) the buses and A Coy 3 & B/W/R Camp 3 in food supply. Very wet morning. Pres. made after dinner & men dried their clothes. Enemy shelled BLANDAIN & near our B.C. Coy during night put no damage.	

WAR DIARY or INTELLIGENCE SUMMARY

Army Form C. 2118.

Place	Date	Hour	Summary of Events and Information	Remarks and references to Appendices
WILLEMS	23/10/15		Remained here during & yesterday & removing shells & other Enemy stores from the dug outs. Great quantities of bomb pigeon lights & found. Also Gravenberghe & bombs with steel decorations & no grit to set bombs or taught how to use. In afternoon CO, IO, & Comp Commanders proceeded to reconnoitre Froyennes to reconnoitre Preparatory to taking over front line from the 217 Kings.	
WILLEMS	24/10		Ordered to relieve 217 Kings today, moved off at 2 P.M. along railway met by Guides at Froyenne. Relief completed by 7.30. A Coy in Right front. D. Coy left front. B Coy in support. C. Coy in Reserve. Three patrols sent during night up to Canal. Capt Marked M.C. & (Butler (R.E.) Reconnoitred East one of these. All patrols encountered	
FROYENNES			Ruin Canal to locate best places to place bridges to crossing in Preparation for advance. Enemy patrol encountered on our Patrol but Retreated across river Canal two deep banks. Enemy M.G. posts fairly close up & active. At 2 P.M. some 40 ft bridging arrived from 505 C. R.E. Gun removed by Artillery during night in front.	

WAR DIARY or INTELLIGENCE SUMMARY.

(Erase heading not required.)

Army Form C. 2118.

Place	Date	Hour	Summary of Events and Information	Remarks and references to Appendices
PROYENNES	25/10/18		Decided to stiffen up right flank which was covered by the 7th Div. Brought up 1 Platoon of Support Coy 3 + 1 M.G. in position to cover the country behind the 7th Div. Posts on right front Coy were also relieved & reorganized. Major C. Biggs (19th Kings) reported to help. He had already been notified re allocated on duty with the battalion. Considerable shelling on French during night. No front posts. Patrols out. Several inhabitants still living in village began up amongst front line.	
"	26/10	11:30 pm	Two men arrived back to HQ of Right Front Platoon wounded. O.C. Coy in order to control the country between the Railway + Canal had placed a Lewis Gun post on the railway before dawn in a crater in embankment. The story given by the two wounded men was very incoherent, but they stated another man had been wounded. A patrol was sent out to obtain news but without success & it was assumed post had moved position. After dark successive patrols were sent out to search. It was not until just before dawn that the Platoon Commander on patrol found the Lewis Gun + magazines, two rifles & one steel helmet but no other trace of the men. (N.B. 3.) Intermittent shelling rather more violent on village + roads during day. Enemy planes very active throughout the night.	

Army Form C. 2118.

WAR DIARY
or
INTELLIGENCE SUMMARY.
(Erase heading not required.)

Place	Date	Hour	Summary of Events and Information	Remarks and references to Appendices
TROYENNES	27/10/18	7 PM	Properties called after having been round left front Coy. "C" Coy. 3 had relieved "D" Coy. 3 here during the night. Photo out all except on extreme front at "C" the canal. More ludging material arrived.	
		2 PM	3 tanks of reserve Brig.? reconnoitred preparatory to taking over here. Pre. N. had to move as Lt Col J.H. Carried out a Recce on house occupied by enemy & faced apparent opposite our B. Coy front. He knew that from the house & enemy had been seen going in & out during day. 40 Rounds by 1 MT Mortar were fired. I never hit on house. L TM fired on Sunken road adjacent occupied by enemy post. 18 P.M. fired bursts of Observed & HE into # TM shelters. P.M.9 also, MG & LG fired to cut off enemy trying to get away. Drainage dam to house Circa N wounded & one B Coy 3 pushed forward & rested house & seized L. Blown identification field not any enemy being found. Man taken was never a very light machine gun by enemy & it to be brought out posts Gully took over Pal MG fire

WAR DIARY or INTELLIGENCE SUMMARY

Army Form C. 2118.

Place	Date	Hour	Summary of Events and Information	Remarks and references to Appendices
FROYENNES	27/10/18		Two Platoons maintained & at 6 P.M party with new P.C. Got into nothing heavily. Considerable Enemy shelling during evening & night on roads around village. M.G. quiet until 4.30 A.M. then active & a rifle whole front patrolled throughout night.	
	28/10		Quiet day. 4.30 P.M. Relieving Battalions began to arrive. 2/4 5 Lancers. Relief complete by 7 P.M. Battalion marched back by Ayes to relieved to billets at CORNET. Enemy shelled Cross Roads S of Railway in FROYENNES but no casualties.	
CORNET	29/10		Made Battalion very comfortable in excellent billets. Men bathed & Morning & afternoon spent in cleaning up & ordered In afternoon C.O. S.O. Comp. 2nd in cmdt moved to Report line & reconnoitre possible positions & chance of advance to Major Biggs ordered to proceed & report for duty to 1/5 R.W.F. Battalion ordered to move back to HELLEMMES - LILLE. Billeting parties set forward Rest or money. Relieved by the 2/3rd London Regt E.C. 2nd Battalion marched to billets at HELLEMMES.	
CORNET	30/10			

THE 9th KING'S

and the part they played in the GREAT ADVANCE.

The recent big advance on the Western front had long been in the minds of those who were to take an active part in it and the chances of its immediate success and its effects on the War generally were the subjects of great deliberation. The 9th Battalion THE KING'S (Liverpool Regiment) T.F under the Command of Lieut Colonel F.W. Ramsay, 2nd Battalion Middlesex Regiment had for three weeks immediately proceeding the advance undergone a vigourous training some distance behind the line with a result that the Battalion was in a very fine condition to undertake the arduous task that would be given to them in the near future. That they would have an important part allotted to them was only to be expected, and at the same time hoped for as they had already established for themselves a very high name for general proficiency and good work in their Brigade. It is only two months ago that in competition with regular Battalions of the Brigade in a Horse Show they were able to take with credit a lion's share of the rewards, while at other sports they are always reckoned a tough proposition to their opponents.

On the night of the 24th September, the Battalion left its reserve billets which it had occupied during the last stages of the preparations for the attack and took up its position in the trenches allotted to it. The weather conditions were extremely bad and a continual deluge of rain quickly churned the the trenches into a quagmire, but even this was not calculated to damp the spirits of the men in the trenches who had braced themselves for a mighty effort and were only conscious of the work to be done and the fact that the Germans would be in retreat on the morrow.

It was known that the 9th King's were to advance in co-operation with the London Scottish, the two Battalions constituting a force known as "Greens Force". This fact alone was sufficient to brace the boys of the 9th for any eventualities in view of the fact that they were to work with a Territorial Battalion that had already created for itself a name. The time for the assault was not communicated to the Battalion until one hour before it was to take place. Our artillery had for the past three days bombarded the enemies lines continuously and the bombardment was renewed on the morning of the 25th at daybreak becoming very intense. At 8-am the 9th King's moved forward towards the first line of British Trenches which had just been vacated by the remaining Battalions of their Brigade, who had now moved forward to the attack on the German Front Line. The enemy were keeping up a hot fire on our attacking force and at this stage in the advance we sustained our first casualties, Major J.W.B. Hunt, 2nd in Command being wounded at about 8-30am. Our communication trenches and front line were during the whole of this time being heavily shelled and all movements were carried out over the open the ground being perfectly flat and affording no cover to the attacking force. At 9-am the Battalion after moving over the open occupied a position immediately behind the old firing line where they remained until 10-am. Several casualties had occured in the Battalion and Companies were now reformed and the position taken up in the open.

between the old firing line and the new support trench, ready for the attack. At 12.15 p.m., the Battalion received orders to advance and attack the German front line, a distance of 600 yards from the British front line. Led by Colonel Ramsay, whose great fortitude and brilliant work had greatly inspired all the Officers and men, the Battalion pushed on eagerly and at 12.30 p.m., the two leading Companies had jumped the front British line and were moving in splendid order towards the German lines. During the whole time that the Battalion were advancing, the enemy maintained a heavy Machine Gun fire on our lines, inflicting many losses in both Officers and men, amongst the number being Major F.S.Evans and Capt H. Howroyd, Commanding "C" and "A" Companies respectively, and Capt. and Adjutant F.S.A.Lederer, all of whom received leg wounds. The latter Officer is very well known in Liverpool Banking circles as the Assistant Manager of the London, City and Midland Bank, Ltd., 4 and 6, Dale Street, Liverpool, and has done very fine work since his appointment as Adjutant of the 9th. King's on the 10th May last. In the face of a very hot fire from the enemy the progress at this stage of the advance was not so pronounced, but at 2.0 p.m. our Machine Guns were brought to play on the enemy's front and this had the effect of reducing considerably the German fire. Our losses had now become very severe but in spite of this the Battalion continued its advance in short rushes and by crawling through the grass and at 3.30 p.m. they had succeeded in establishing themselves in one line within 100 yards of the German trenches. The London Scottish now came up to their support on the left rear. At 3.55 p.m. the Germans surrendered to the King's who had stuck to their work with great tenacity and were rewarded by the capture of some 300 to 400 prisoners, Colonel Ramsay, who had led his men with great dash and spirit, receiving the token of submission from the now shrinking Huns who had once more shown their fear and dread of the British bayonet. The prisoners were quickly sent to the rear and the Battalion again reformed with orders to advance on the remaining lines of German trenches and at 4.30 p.m., the Battalion, its strength then being 5 Officers and 130 men took up a position on the ....Road. This position was maintained until 4 a.m. on the morning of the 26th when orders were received to retire on the first line of German trenches, the Brigade having been relieved and here the Battalion remained during the whole of the day and the following night. On the morning of the 27th we were again withdrawn to the original British line where we remained until the early morning of the 29th. The 25th September will ever be remembered in the 9th Battalion "THE KING'S" as a day of acievements. On this day another testimony was given to justify the good name that the Battalion has always enjoyed under the Command of Colonel Ramsay.

On the 29th September the Battalion left the
trenches and moved into billets some three miles
behind the line, the general opinion among the
men being that they were now to receive a well
earned rest. Accordingly they settled down to
take things easy for a little while, but at 7 p.m.
the same night orders were received to proceed to
hold a section of the trenches recently captured
from the enemy in the South East of the village of
L.....   At 9 p.m. the Battalion left their
billets and in a deluge of rain marched back to
the line in splendid spirits in spite of the fatigue
resulting from the recent heavy fighting. This line
was held until the night of the 1st October and
during the whole of the time the enemy's artillery
was very active and our line was shelled incessantly.
We were relieved late on the night of 1st and
marched to billets at .....   After a week's hard
fighting the Battalion were now able to obtain a
well earned rest and at the same time take advantage
of the few days at their disposal to re-organise
and re-fit in readiness for the next engagement.
On 4th October moving orders were again received
and the same evening our former billets some three
miles behind the line were again occupied by the
Battalion until the evening of the 6th.   On the
6th the Battalion was temporarily attached to the
...... Brigade and orders were received to take over
a portion in of their line north of the village of
L..... It was found necessary to at once carry
out extensive digging operations, the trenches being
extremely shallow and offering no cover to the fire
of the enemy's artillery which was very active.
At about 10.30 a.m . on the morning of the 8th the
enemy's artillery opened fire on our frontline and
support trenches and maintained a steady fire
throughout the day with great accuracy, the fire
evidently being directed by a hostile aeroplane
which remained over us for some time. Considerable
damage was done to our line during the bombardment
but at 2.30 p.m. it became terrific, the enemy
guns enfilading our trenches from the North and
South East.   At 3.30 p.m. the enemy also concen-
trated Machine Gun and rifle fire on our front and
the Battalion sustained very heavy casualties. At
3.50 p.m. the Germans advanced to the attack in
mass, marching in four ranks shoulder to shoulder.
In spite of the severe losses already suffered, the
remaining men in the front line trenches stuck to
their posts with great tenacity, but it was found
necessary to reinforce the front line from the
Supports.   The enemy advance, which was strongly
supported, having reached mid-way between the lines,
were now met with a rapid rifle and cross Machine
Gun fire, the Germans falling in great numbers.
The enemy had been severely checked and small groups
could now be seen endeavouring to regain their own
line in great disorder under a hot fire from our
Machine Guns and rifles. During the attack the
enemy succeeded in establishing a very intense "tir
de barrage" of shrapnel, H.E. and Machine Guns, and
the casualties in our front line were by this time
very heavy further reinforcements being brought up
on the flanks.   At about 5 p.m. our Artillery
obtained superiority of fire and this had the effect
of reducing the enemy fire considerably. At this
period of the fight, the Battalion had not more
than 300 rifles holding the line but the spirits

of the men was magnificent, even the wounded who
were unable to leave the trench cheering their
comrades with shouts of "Go it "The King's", "Stick
it King's, give it them hot". Worn out but not
dismayed the Battalion, or what then remained, still
held on and bravely carried out Colonel Ramsay's
command to "keep cheerful". At 8.15 p.m. a company
of the London Scottish came up as reinforcements
and the situation became slightly easier, the enemy
making no further attempt to attack the position
again that night. At 5 a.m. the following morning
the Battalion was withdrawn into the old British
Support line, having finished a terrific day, and
were rewarded for their fine work by congratulations
from the G.O's C the Corps, Division and Brigade.

For the second time in a fortnight, the
9th King's had been called upon to play an important
part in the advance on the Western front, and on
each occasion they have carried out their part with
great credit to their Colonel, themselves and the
"KING'S" Regiment.

The following "SPECIAL ORDER OF THE DAY"
by Major-General A.E.A. Holland. C.B., M.V.O., D.S.O
Commanding ... Division, was issued and received
by Colonel Ramsay on the 10th October:-

"The Corps Commander has desired
"the General Officer Commanding to
"convey to the General Officer
"Commanding ... Infantry Brigade,
"and all ranks under his Command,
"his appreciation of the gallant
"defence made by the brigade against
"the German attack on the 8th instant,
"and especially the good work done
"by the 1st Battalion Gloucestershire
"Regiment and the 1/9th Battalion
"Liverpool Regiment."

(signed) B. Tulloch.
Lieut.Colonel.
A.A.G.&.M.G. ... Division.

WAR DIARY or INTELLIGENCE SUMMARY

Army Form C. 2118.

12/57 B. Stevens Lt.Col.

Battalion 7th King's (Liverpool Regt) T.F.

Place	Date	Hour	Summary of Events and Information	Remarks and references to Appendices
HELLEMMES	30/10/18		The Battalion arrived in HELLEMMES at 20.30 hours and marched into billets which consisted of a large factory. Every man being supplied with a bed. The officers were billeted in private houses in the vicinity.	
	31/10/18		The morning was spent in cleaning up billets and vicinity thereof. Afternoon the men had the remainder of the day for rest. At 16.0 Adjt & Coy Cmdrs reconnoitred to training areas which were to be used by the Battalion during the time in this area. Orders were received from Bde HQrs that 1 hour per day would be devoted to training rt, and the remainder of the day for Recreation and organised games. The area was found to be very extensive and most adaptable for everyone. Dug & Critical schemes. Also every facility was found for Rifle & Lewis gun firing & Rifle Grenade firing.	
	1/11/18		The Battalion commenced their training this day, the following programme being carried out :- The Coys on the Rifle Range Lewis Gun Range practising & handling of arms.	

WAR DIARY
or
INTELLIGENCE SUMMARY.

Army Form C. 2118.

Place	Date Nov.	Hour	Summary of Events and Information	Remarks and references to Appendices
HELLEMMES	1/11/18		Usual Bill to and ceremonial drill.	
	2/11/18		Training as for previous day was again carried out	
	3/11/18		Divine service took place in the billets occupied by the Battn. The first floor of the factory was in question that it was decided to hold the Brigade service, there being sufficient accommodation for the whole of the Brigade Personnel	
	4/11/18 5/11/18 6/11/18 7/11/18		The usual training was carried out on each of these days	
			The usual inspections and training again took place. During the morning the Brigade Commander inspected the Battalion in full marching order.	
	8/11/18 9/11/18 10/11/18		The training was again carried on. Divine Service was again held on the first floor of the factory. The whole of the Brigade Personnel attending as previously	
	11/11/18		The usual training was carried out. In the morning of the 11th Official news was received that an armistice had been signed for duration of 36 days. Before marching off from the parade ground the C.O. addressed all ranks informing them of the historical event.	
	12/11/18		The usual training was again carried out.	

WAR DIARY or INTELLIGENCE SUMMARY

Army Form C. 2118.

Place	Date	Hour	Summary of Events and Information	Remarks and references to Appendices
HELLEMMES	23/11/18		An inspection took place in full marching order by the G.O.C. Division. The inspection was followed by a ceremonial march past by the night of the 13th way to reply to the Armistice was shown by the returning of British Prisoners of War noted from the Germans lines. A bugler was sent immediately these men they were escorted into billets which had been prepared for them. Fires were burning and every man was supplied with a hot meal after which Tea and a Rum ration was served to them as they arrived. By midnight about 80 men had arrived. Many of the men arriving in an exhausted condition after having marched 40/50 kilos. It was a touching sight to see these men who referred to many defence regiments. Many were stirring picture Souls, related by these repatriated men of British of the harsh + cruel treatment which they received during their period of Captivity. The usual training was again carried out. Orders were received during the morning that the returning Prisoners of War should be forwarded to the XI Corps Reception Camp. Lr Colonel Abale M.C. proceeded on leave. Lr Colonel B. Deaxton of the 2nd Br ALR reported for duty and took	

D.D. & L., London, E.C. (A501) Wt. W1771/M2931 750,000 5/17 Sch. 53 Forms/C2118/14

WAR DIARY
or
INTELLIGENCE SUMMARY.

Army Form C. 2118.

(Erase heading not required.)

Place	Date	Hour	Summary of Events and Information	Remarks and references to Appendices
HELLEMMES	14/4/16		Took Command of the Battalion.	
	15/4/16 17/4/16		The Battalion carried out an "Advance Guard" Tactical Scheme. Major Begg M.C. of the 19th Liverpool Regt reported for duty as 2nd in Command. Representatives of the Regimental Institute who commenced also Menus for Sergts Offrs & a Bn Mens Mess was [ ] A/Coy Institute. He Scheme met with great success when tried.) A Recreation room was also made which proved most popular and several Bato Concerts hence were held.	
	18/4/16 19/4/16		The usual training was carried out. The Battalion took part in a Cross Country run against the 9th S.L.R. It was decided that a medal should be provided by the G.O.C.L.R. if the winner were tried to be a 9th SLR man since proved to be Kilmarnock. After a well contested race the winner proved to be 2/L Kilmarnock of B Coy of this Battalion.	
	20/4/16 21/4/16		The usual training was carried out.	
	22/4/16		The Battalion carried out a route march.	

WAR DIARY or **INTELLIGENCE SUMMARY**

Army Form C. 2118.

Place	Date	Hour	Summary of Events and Information	Remarks and references to Appendices
HELLEMMES	23/11/18		The usual training was again carried out. 100, to whole of the firing parties to the Factory. No again 100, to whole of the Brigade personnel taking part.	
	28/11/18		Educational Classes were arranged under the supervision of the Educational Officer, Revd. R.J. Briggs. The following subjects were taken:- Drawing; Drawing; Simple reading & writing lessons: Geography; Shorthand; French. On the morning of assembly, a large number of the Batt- -alion's arrived themselves of the opportunity of undoubtedly gain knowledge of subjects which will undoubtedly prove beneficial to them on their returning to their civilian occupation. Half of the other ranks arrived to join the Battalion. the general appearance & fitness of these men was very satisfactory. The usual training was again carried out. R.S.M. reports for duty	
	28/11/18		Lt. Colonel McMahyle - Buchler - Mailand, R.C.O assumed command of the Unit	
	29/11/18		The usual training Educational classes were again carried out. A warning order was received this day that the Battalion would be moving to ETRUN about the 3rd of Dec by route march the two days, during this march Lieut. CARVIN with the Advanced liner for one night. An advance preceded to ETRUN to prepare	

Army Form C. 2118.

WAR DIARY
or
INTELLIGENCE SUMMARY.
(Erase heading not required.)

Instructions regarding War Diaries and Intelligence Summaries are contained in F. S. Regs., Part II. and the Staff Manual respectively. Title pages will be prepared in manuscript.

Place	Date	Hour	Summary of Events and Information	Remarks and references to Appendices
HELLEMMES	28 & 29/4/19		The billeting accommodation for the arrival of the Battalion. The usual training, also Educational classes, were again carried out.	
	30/4/19		The Battalion carried out a route march during the period. During the month, a Divisional Football Competition has been held, the Battalion finishing up with three successive victories. There has also been an officer's tug of war completion, this Battalion team having won 2 matches out of 2 played, and so now eligible to play in the Semi-finals.	

Walker
Lieut. Col.
Cmdg. 9th Bn. The King's

Army Form C. 2118.

WAR DIARY
or
INTELLIGENCE SUMMARY

9th Bn. "THE KING'S" (L'POOL REGT) T.F.

(Erase heading not required.)

9th Batn. The Kings (Pool Regt) T.F. 1918

Place	Date	Hour	Summary of Events and Information	Remarks and references to Appendices
HELLEMMES	Nov 1st		Brigade Divine Service was held in this unit.	Q.6.a.50. Sheet 36.SE
	1,2,3		Training as follows, was carried out on ground allotted this unit:- Musketry, Lewis Guns, B. & P.T. Close Order Drill, Handling of Arms etc., & Section & Platoon. One hour each morning.	
	3.4		The Battalion moved by Route March to CARVIN, en route for new billeting Area, i.e., ETRUN.	
CARVIN	4th		The Battalion moved from CARVIN, arriving in its new ETRUN, about 15.30 hours. The distance (covered) on the day was roughly 21 miles; the notable feature of the march being,— not a single file was out on line of march, which reflects great credit on those responsible for the training of the Battalion.	L.1.98.80 (LENS.II)
ETRUN	5th		The morning was spent in cleaning up of Billets etc. afterwards, the remainder of the day was placed at the disposal of the men for their own recreation	23.g

WAR DIARY
or
INTELLIGENCE SUMMARY.

9th Bn. "THE KING'S" (L'POOL REGT) T.F.

Place	Date	Hour	Summary of Events and Information	Remarks and references to Appendices
ETRUN	Nov 6th		9th Battalion The King's L'pool Regt T.F.	
			The usual training was carried out.	3.I. 30. 85. (Lens 11)
	7th		The Battalion was inspected in full marching Order by the Commanding Officer. Lieut Col Harlow DSO. Divine Service (Voluntary)	
	8th			
	9th		The Battalion moved from billets in ETRUN to "E" Block Y. Huts near ARRAS - SAINT POL ROAD Battalion Hd qrs being established at 3.I. 30. 50. (LENS. 11)	3.I. 30. 50. (LENS. 11)
Y Huts	10th		The usual training was carried out.	
	11th		A route march was contemplated but owing to the inclement weather postponement was necessary	
	12th		The usual training was carried out.	
	13th		The usual training was carried out. The initial intimation of Demobilization was received from Brigade own instructions being to dispatch to the nearest Minefields & miners for demobilization. This allotment was the forerunner of many to come.	
	14th		The Battalion was inspected in full marching Order by the Brig. Genl. "B" Coy being declared the smartest turned out Coy, their reward being a holiday on the following	

Army Form C. 2118.

WAR DIARY
INTELLIGENCE SUMMARY
(Erase heading not required.)

Instructions regarding War Diaries and Intelligence Summaries are contained in F. S. Regs., Part II. and the Staff Manual respectively. Title pages will be prepared in manuscript.

HEADQUARTERS
9th BN. "THE KING'S"
("POOL" REGT.) L.F.

(3)

9th Battalion The King's (L'pool Regt.) L.F.

Place	Date	Hour	Summary of Events and Information	Remarks and references to Appendices
Y. Hutmerle	14th		Thursday, - a trip to DOULLENS by motor lorry.	
"	15th		A further 12 miners were despatched to England on this day for Demobilization. Divine Service was held.	
"	16th		The usual Training was carried out	
"	17th		The usual Training was carried out	
"	18th		A route march had to be postponed on this day owing to the inclement weather.	
"	19th		The usual Training was carried out.	
"	20th		The usual Training was carried out.	
"	21st		The Battalion was inspected by the Commander's Officer. (Lieut.Col. Maitland D.S.O.) One miner was despatched to England for Demobilization.	
"	22nd		Divine Service was held.	
"	23rd		The usual Training was carried out.	
"	24th		The usual Training was carried out.	
"	25th		Christmas Day. Divine Service was held at 11.00 hours. Dinner was served to the Battalion at 18.00 hours,	

WAR DIARY

Army Form C. 2118.

INTELLIGENCE SUMMARY.
(Erase heading not required.)

9th Battalion The King's (Liverpool Regt) 1/7

HEADQUARTERS
9th BN. "THE KING'S"
L'POOL REGT. 1.F

Place	Date	Hour	Summary of Events and Information	Remarks and references to Appendices
T. Helmet	Dec 25th		The menu consisted of :- Roast Pork - Roast Beef - Vegetables - Apple Sauce - Plum Pudding - DESSERT :- Nuts. Apples - Rum Punch. & Beer. The arrangements for the festivity were excellently carried out, the fare provided was greatly relished & appreciated by the men. A Battalion run was organized. Lots Dec at	
	26th	11.00 hours. Every available man was on the parade. At 18.00 hours the Sergeants held their Christmas Dinner, also men who were on employ on Xmas Day were also provided with the special Xmas fare In the evening the Officers held their Xmas festivity. A route march orders for the day was reluctantly	
	27th		abandoned, owing to inclement weather. Lieut. Colonel Ramsdens D.S.O. reports for duty with the Battalion.	
	28th		Lieut Colonel Ramsdens D.S.O. assumes Command of the Battalion, vice Lieut Colonel Mullens, who proceeds to Command 2nd Guards Battalion.	

Army Form C. 2118.

HEADQUARTERS
DATE
9th BN. "THE KING'S" (L'POOL REGT.) T.F.

WAR DIARY
INTELLIGENCE SUMMARY

9th Battalion The King's (L'pool) Regt. 11/17

Place	Date	Hour	Summary of Events and Information	Remarks and references to Appendices
Y. Huts	Dec. 29th		Divine Service was held.	
	30th		The usual Training was carried out. Major E.H. Riches M.C. proceeded to the Army Staff Camp as 2nd in Command.	
	31st		The usual Training was carried out. The fighting strength of the Battalion on the 31st was 27 Officers, 658. O. Ranks.	

F H Mess
Lieut Colonel
Commanding 9th Bn The King's (L'pool) Regt. T.F.

In the Field
5.1.1919

Army Form C. 2118.

WAR DIARY
or
INTELLIGENCE SUMMARY.
(Erase heading not required.)

Jan 1919

Place	Date	Hour	Summary of Events and Information	Remarks and references to Appendices
MARŒUIL Y Huts OKHS L2 C and d.	1919 Jan 1st & 2nd		Divisional Race Meeting held on ARRAS Racecourse. The Battalion was given a holiday on both days to attend the races. The Battalion entered three horses and one mule. None of these were placed in the events they were entered for. On Jan 2nd Colours Party left the Battn. to bring the Regimental Colours from the Depot in LIVERPOOL. The Colour Party was composed as follows :- Lieut F. FISHER " H.T SPARGO 332380 Sergt MORGAN.J.F. D.C.M. M.M. 330073 " PENNINGTON.J. M.M. 332044 Corpl TAYLOR.J. M.M.	See A.F. 51 C.
	3		Usual training carried out.	
	4		Two other ranks left the Battn. for demobilization during the week making a total of 23 in all.	
	5.		Sunday. Church Parades. C.O. inspected Transport.	
	6		Lieut Col Lord HENRY C. SEYMOUR D.S.O. his Major S.C. BALL D.S.O. mentioned in despatches	
	7-10		Usual training. Each Company or Section once down to week.	
	11		Battn. Route March. Colour Party returned from England. Regimental Colours put in Centre Room, Officers Mess. The Colours were presented to the Battn. by the Lord Mayor of Liverpool on 7th Jan.	Appendix I

Army Form C. 2118.

WAR DIARY
INTELLIGENCE SUMMARY.
(Erase heading not required.)

Instructions regarding War Diaries and Intelligence Summaries are contained in F. S. Regs., Part II. and the Staff Manual respectively. Title pages will be prepared in manuscript.

Place	Date 1919	Hour	Summary of Events and Information	Remarks and references to Appendices
MAROEUIL Ytrainements L2 C and 8	Jan. 11		One officer and 16 other ranks left the Battn. for demobilisation, making up a total of one officer (Capt. J L LEE-JONES) and 39 other ranks.	See Sheet S.I.C.
	12		Sunday Church Parades.	
	13		Meeting held in Recreation Room re formation of 55th Division Comrades Association. 73 all ranks joined the association.	
	14-17		Usual training and salvage.	
	18		Whole Battn. on Salvage. One officer (2/Lieut E J WAYMARK) and 46 other Ranks left Battn. for demobilisation making a total of two officers and 85 other Ranks. Team of winners stamps gave a demonstration of Musketry.	
	19		Sunday. Church Parades. Battn. boxing tournament held in the afternoon.	
	20th 21st 22nd		"C" Company artificial no answers of Brigade Boxing Competition. Brigade Boxing Tournament held at ECOIVRES. The Battn. entered four Novices and won two contests. the Divisional Commander inspected the camp in the morning and congratulated the C.O. on the camp, workshops etc.	
	23		Forms Ggs other dated 18th Jan. received authorising transfer of M.S.M. to 53221 Sergt. GRAHAM N.H. and 331169 Corpl KYNASTON. H.	
	25		Civic Country Run won by "B" Company. 39 other ranks left battn. during the week making a total of 3 officers and 124 other ranks.	

Army Form C. 2118.

WAR DIARY
or
INTELLIGENCE SUMMARY.
(Erase heading not required.)

Place	Date	Hour	Summary of Events and Information	Remarks and references to Appendices
MARŒUIL Y Mines 15 L2c/d.	26 27th 31		Sunday. Moved training and Salvage carried out. Strength of Battalion 3 Officers 615 Other Ranks. Fighting Strength 34 " 611 " Available Fighting Strength 24 " 360 " Total all ranks demobilised to date 3 Officers 151 Other Ranks.	

J M Jew hart Col.
Commanding
4th Batt. The Keir p April 1921

APPENDIX I

EXTRACT FROM THE "LIVERPOOL DAILY POST & MERCURY" dated 7-1-19.

THE 9th's COLOURS:
Presentation Ceremony at the Town Hall.

A stirring military spectacle was witnessed on the Exchange Flags today, the occasion being the ceremony of restoring to the 9th Battalion THE "KING'S" (Liverpool) Regiment the colours deposited at the Town Hall before the Battalion went to the war in 1915.

The actual handing-over of the colours by the Lord Mayor to the escort of the Battalion sent from France to receive them took place in the Town Hall, and afterwards the escort carried them to the Exchange Flags, and joined the guard of honour furnished by the 3rd Border Regiment.

A large gathering of the public was present on the Flags, The Lord Mayor was accompanied by the Lady Mayoress, and amongst the Officers present were Colonel Lloyd (Who commanded the Battalion when it went to France in 1915) Colonel Bond, Colonel Perry, Majors Evans, DSO, Nairn, Ledere, and Wells, Captains Howroyd (Commanding Officer at the Depot of the 9th Battalion, in Everton Road) Perry, (Who has just returned from captivity in Germany) Daniels, and Buckley; and Lieut. Harold S. Heenan. There was a good attendance of discharged non-commissioned officers and men of the 9th Battalion, which was originally the PRESS GUARDS.

The battalion is at present outside ARRAS, and the escort which consisted of Lieutenants Fisher and Spargo, and three non-commissioned officers, will convey the colours there. The colours were of the suctomary description - the King's flag and the Regimental Flag.

The Band of the 3rd Battalion Border Regiment played selections of music before the ceremony.

The Lord Mayor, having presented the colours to the escort delivered a speech. That was the fourth time, he said, he had the opportunity of saying "Good-bye" to the colours of local regiments.

Being an old Volunteer Officer himself, he had a warm feeling towards the Territorials, as he had had more to do with them than with the Regular Army.

The 9th Battalion had done splendidly at the front in upholding the honour of their regiment and the credit of their town. They went out in 1915 and had gone through a very good share of the fighting, including the Somme in 1916.

The battalion had added lustre to its great reputation, which he was sure would be worthily maintained in future. He wished them a very speedy return home to Liverpool.

The escort and guard of honour then marched from the Exchange Flags to Lime-Street Station, via Castle Street, Lord Street, Church Street, and Elliott Street.

Army Form C. 2118.

WAR DIARY or INTELLIGENCE SUMMARY.

(Erase heading not required.)

Instructions regarding War Diaries and Intelligence Summaries are contained in F.S. Regs., Part II. and the Staff Manual respectively. Title pages will be prepared in manuscript.

HEADQUARTERS
DATE ... March ...
5th Bn. Th'E KING'S
(L'POOL REGT) T.F.

Place	Date	Hour	Summary of Events and Information	Remarks and references to Appendices
"Y" HUTMENTS MAROEUIL	1919 Mar 1 2.(Sun)		The usual programme of training was carried out. Brigade service held in Battalion Recreation Hut. The Senior Chaplain (C of E) 57th Division conducted the service.	
	3.		13 Other Ranks left the Battalion for demobilization. The whole Battalion on fatigue.	
	4.		30 other ranks left the Battalion for demobilization. Lieut Colonel J.O. Du Pres D.S.O. assumed command of the 172nd Infantry Bde during the temporary absence of the Brig General. Usual programme of training was carried out. 1 Officer (Lieut. H. Bickley) & 7 other ranks left the Battalion for demobilization.	
	5.		Battalion employed on Brigade duties. 16 other ranks left the Battalion for demobilization.	
	6.		The whole of the Battalion employed on fatigue. Captain R.C. Heywood M.C. & 7/Lieut. J.S. Wray left the Battalion for demobilization.	
	7.		Battalion programme of training carried out. Lieut Wray proceeded for demob. Lieut Colonel J.O. Du Pres D.S.O. relinquished command of the 172nd Infantry Bde.	
	8.		Usual programme of training was carried out. 3 other ranks left the Battalion for demobilization. also 3 Officers namely Lieut M. J. Wallace, 2/Lt R.H. Anwell & 2/Lieut J. Telford.	

WAR DIARY or INTELLIGENCE SUMMARY

Army Form C. 2118.

HEADQUARTERS
9th Bn. "THE KING'S" (L'POOL REGT) T.F.

Place	Date	Hour	Summary of Events and Information	Remarks and references to Appendices
"Y" HUTMENTS MAROEUIL	1919 Dec. 9 (Sun)		Brigade service held in this Battalion's lines. Battalion other ranks proceeded for demobilization.	
	10.		No 14 Platoon of "A" Company completed in the Brigade Platoon Competition but was beaten by a Platoon of the Royal Munster Fusiliers. The Battalion was employed on Brigade duties	
	11.		Usual programme of training carried out.	
	12.		Baths and Brigade duties.	
	13.		The whole battalion employed on salvage.	
	14.		15 other ranks left the battalion for demobilization. Battalion employed on Brigade duties.	
	15.		Baths. Usual programme of training. 3 Other ranks left the battalion for demobilization	
	16.(Sun)		Brigade Divine held in this Battalion's lines.	
	17.		The whole battalion employed on Salvage. 12 Other ranks proceeded for demobilization	
	18.		The battalion employed on Brigade duties	
	19.		" " " "	
	20.		6 Other ranks left the battalion to proceed for demobilization	
	21.		Battalion employed on Brigade duties	

Army Form C. 2118.

HEADQUARTERS
1/10 Bn. "THE KING'S"
(L'POOL REGT.) T.F.

WAR DIARY
or
INTELLIGENCE SUMMARY.
(Erase heading not required.)

Instructions regarding War Diaries and Intelligence Summaries are contained in F. S. Regs., Part II. and the Staff Manual respectively. Title pages will be prepared in manuscript.

Place	Date	Hour	Summary of Events and Information	Remarks and references to Appendices
"Y" HUTMENTS MARDEUIL	1919 22		Bugle Notice	
	23 (Sun)		Brigade Service held in Battalion's Lines.	
	24, 25.		Brigade duties	
	26.		Brigade duties. 15 Other ranks left the Battalion for demobilization.	
	27.		3 Officers namely Capt. Long, Roberts MC, Lieut N. Longo, 2/Lieut J H Pyke 4 45 Other ranks left the battalion to join the 5th Division	
			A draft of 30 Officers to the Army of Occupation. 18 Other ranks proceeded for demobilization	
	28.		Brigade duties	

F. H. Drew
Lieut Colonel
Comog. 9th Battalion "The King's" L'pool Regt T.F.

Army Form C. 2118.

WAR DIARY
or
INTELLIGENCE SUMMARY.
(Erase heading not required.)

HEADQUARTERS
9th Bn. "THE KING'S" (L'POOL REGT) T.F.

Instructions regarding War Diaries and Intelligence Summaries are contained in F. S. Regs., Part II. and the Staff Manual respectively. Title pages will be prepared in manuscript.

Place	Date	Hour	Summary of Events and Information	Remarks and references to Appendices
"HUTMENTS" MAROEUIL	MAR 1919 1.		The Battalion had the use of the Brigade Baths. Brigade Church Service held in the Recreation Room of the Battalion. Battalion employed on salvage	
	2.		" " "	
	3.		" " "	
	4.		" " "	
	5.		" " "	
	6.		" " "	
	7.		29 Other ranks left the Battalion for demobilization. Lt. D. Roberts, MC commanded this party	
	8.		Battalion route march	
	9.		Brigade Service held in the Recreation Room of this Battalion. The Divisional Chaplain conducted the service	
	10.		The Battalion took part in the Royal Brigade Knock Out Competition against the 4th Bn. South Lancs Regt. & after a well contested game won by 2 goals to nil. Brig General Pryper presented the medals after the match.	
	11.		The Battalion had the use of the Brigade Baths	
	12.		Lieut Col J.G.W. Burns DSO assumes Command of the 1/9 th Kings Bn. during the temporary absence of the Brig. General commanding	
	13.14.15		Battalion employed on salvage	

WAR DIARY
INTELLIGENCE SUMMARY

9th Bn. "THE KING'S" (L'POOL REGT.) T.F.

Army Form C. 2118.

Place	Date	Hour	Summary of Events and Information	Remarks and references to Appendices
MARQUEL	MAR 16		Bugscall dances in the Recreation Room of the Battalion.	
	17, 18		Battalion employed on salvage.	
	19		Battalion attended a lecture in the Recreation Room given by Capt. E.G. Bohrer 2nd Bn. London Regt. SUBJECT "The army after the War".	
	20		11 men left the Battalion for demobilization. The Battalion employed on salvage.	
	21, 22		The Battalion employed on salvage.	
	23, 24		A voluntary non-compulsory rural was held in the Battalion lines. The Battalion was employed in moving the Sanreport to the vicinity of "B" "Y" Huttments.	
	25		do	
	26		Lieut. C.G. Rigby 9/16 (R.O) to weck hence left the Battalion for demobilization. Capt. B.K. (R.O) proceeded to join the 25th Bn Kings L'pool Regt for the carrying on of Occupation. 2nd/Lieut. F.G. Burrows continues to take charge.	
	27, 28		2 O.Rs left the Battalion for demobilization. Capt. Col. F. Hill MC. Lieut. H.M. Wagnall MC & 2/Lt. E. Birchwood proceeded for demobilization. Battalion employed on salvage.	
	29		Capt. A.S. 42. Allen Ranks proceeded to join the 25 Bn Kings L'pool Regt for Army of Occupation. 2nd/Lieut W.B. Rep concluded the charge.	
	30		Capt. Col. W.D.G. Drew DSO proceeded on 7 days leave to Ireland. Bugscall Dances held in Recreation Room of the Battalion. The Battalion practically reduced to about 20% of the personnel required to carry out Battalion duties.	

WAR DIARY
or
INTELLIGENCE SUMMARY.

Army Form C. 2118.

HEADQUARTERS
9th Bn. "THE KING'S"
(L'POOL. REGT.) T.F.

Place	Date	Hour	Summary of Events and Information	Remarks and references to Appendices
Harwich	1-30 Apr		The Battalion now being reduced to Cadre Strength, the whole of the personnel have been employed during the month upon Battalion duties. Each Sunday during the month a Church Service for the Brigade was held in the Recreation Room of this Battalion. On the 5th of the month, Brigadier General G. Paynter D.S.O. visited the Battalion to bid farewell. All available Officers & Other Ranks paraded, and the Brigadier shook hands with each individual. During the month the Battalion has had an allotment each week for the Brigade baths.	

B.J.Shaw.
Captain for
Lieut Colonel Commanding
9th Bn "The King's" (L'pool R'gt) T.F.

WAR DIARY
or
INTELLIGENCE SUMMARY

Army Form C. 2118.

HEADQUARTERS
9th Battalion "THE KING'S"
(LIVERPOOL REGT.) T.F.

Place	Date	Hour	Summary of Events and Information	Remarks and references to Appendices
Mesourt			The whole of this month the personnel of the Bn. were employed in Battalion duties. Church parade was held each Sunday in the Battalion lines.	
	10/5/1919		The Commanding Officer - Lieut Colonel 3rd W. Picco D.S.O. having been appointed Commander of No 61 Prisoner Group left the Battalion on the 10th. The whole of the personnel of the Bn. paraded to wish him farewell and he shook hands with each individual. Major Scobell took over command of the unit on this day.	

C.B. Nixon
Capt. for
Major Commanding

57 DIVISION

172 BDE

2/9 BN KINGS LIVERPOOL REGT
1915 SEP — 1916 FEB
1917 FEB — 1918 JAN

ABSORBED BY 9 BN

www.ingramcontent.com/pod-product-compliance
Lightning Source LLC
Chambersburg PA
CBHW081436160426
43193CB00013B/2296